A BIRDWATCHING GUIDE TO
MOROCCO

PETE COMBRIDGE
ALAN SNOOK

ARLEQUIN

ISBN 1 900159 65 1

First published 1997

Arlequin Press, 26 Broomfield Road, Chelmsford, Essex CM1 1SW
Telephone: 01245 267771
© Text and Maps, Pete Combridge & Alan Snook
© Front cover and Line Drawings, James McCallum
© Photographs, as credited

All rights reserved. No part of this book may be reproduced, stored in a retrieval system or transmitted in any form or by any means, electronic, mechanical, photocopying or otherwise, without the permission of the publisher.

A catalogue record for this book is available.

CONTENTS

Acknowledgements 4

Introduction 5

Getting there and other tips 5

Bibliography 9

Key to maps 10

Site Guides 12

Useful addresses 42

Checklists 43

Acknowledgements

The authors would like to thank Mike Combridge for permission to use his photographs, Lawrence Chappell for support early in the project, James McCallum for his excellent line drawings and cover illustration, and, last but not least, our wives Sue and Julie for their patience.

Introduction

Even today, when travel to remote places can sometimes seem commonplace, Morocco, with its often magnificent scenery and characterful people, remains an exciting and interesting country to visit. For the birdwatcher it holds not only a good range of endemic species, and true rarities such as the Bald Ibis, but also easy access to several sought-after desert dwellers.

This guide is aimed primarily at those with limited time, who wish to cover a cross section of habitats and find a good selection of species. It therefore concentrates on the most easily accessible parts of the Kingdom. We intend to update this guide at intervals, so any comments, corrections, changes or new sites for possible inclusion will be gratefully received. All contributions will of course be acknowledged in any future edition.

Getting there and other tips

Visitors contemplating long stays could well consider bringing their own transport from Europe, with the ferries which run from Algeciras and Gibraltar probably the most convenient.

Travellers with limited time will probably arrive by air, and there are plenty of International flights, both scheduled and chartered, and six major airports to choose from (see map 1). Agadir and Marrakech provide pretty good all-round entry points for most birding trips, and Agadir also provides a good package holiday destination for birdwatching purposes.

Visa requirements can change, but currently British Passport holders do not require one for visits of less than three months. The usual pre-trip health precautions should be taken; your doctor will advise.

Credit cards are of little use away from main cities and tourist areas. Note that it is advisable to finish the trip with as little Moroccan currency (Dirhams) as possible, as there is a limit to the amount you can change back. The airport banks (if open!) often have a limited range and supply of foreign currency available, and it is not allowed to export Dirhams. At present no departure tax is charged.

Getting around

If time is limited, by far the most convenient way of getting around is by hire car. Whilst these are undeniably expensive, they do allow you access to areas tricky or impossible by public transport. Moroccan hire cars are not renown for being in the best of condition, so be sure to check everything checkable (tyres, tool kit, etc) before driving off. One of the authors of this guide was half way up the High Atlas before discovering that the handbrake of his hire car did not work!

The traffic is usually light and the roads of good standard, but they can be rough in places and of little more than one vehicle width. If another vehicle is coming at you from the other direction, it will be prudent to give way – the chances are he won't! As in many other countries, don't expect any traffic rules to be followed and take great care at night; don't expect other vehicles to have lights, and watch for people and animals walking out in front of you in populated areas. Accidents or breakdowns are often marked by stones placed in the road, and these are easy to miss at night. Before you cancel your trip after all these daunting cautions, we can say that having driven in many other parts of the world, Morocco is really pretty straightforward and should present little problem to an experienced driver.

For route finding we can recommend with confidence the Michelin Road Map 969, and therefore the guide follows the place name spellings used by Michelin in the text.

Weather

Whilst the summers are very hot, the winters, although less severe than northern Europe, can nevertheless be cold and wet. The passes through the Atlas can be blocked at times with snow; you may have to wait for a snowplough! In short, for a winter trip it's worth bringing waterproofs and warm clothing, especially in and around the Atlas.

The following graphs of temperature and rainfall for five scattered localities will hopefully give you an idea of what to expect at different times of year.

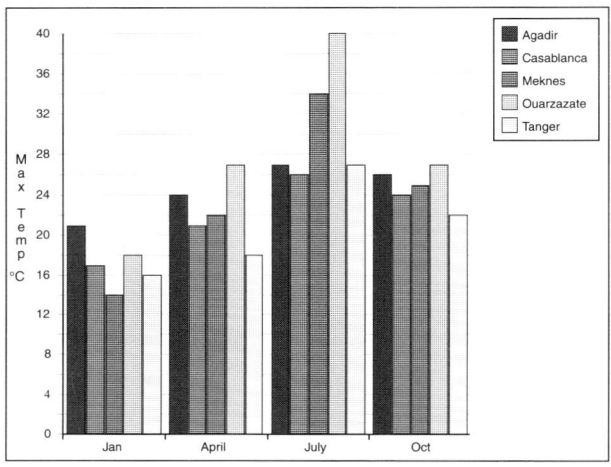

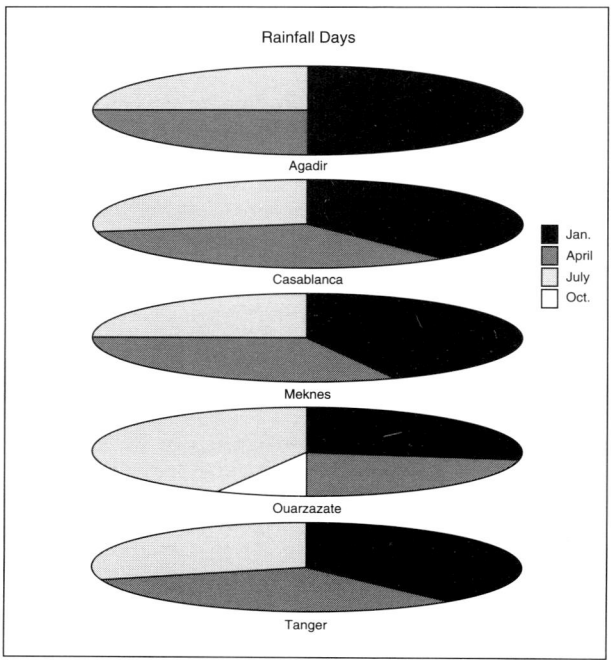

Accommodation

If you are on a tight budget there are many relatively cheap and clean hotels available. Don't expect such luxuries as hot water (maybe lukewarm or intermittent) or towels. Nonetheless they are good value. It is beyond the scope of this book to delve too deeply into this subject, so we unreservedly recommend the *Rough Guide* (see bibliography) as a generally invaluable aid to finding suitable hotels. Other such travel guides are sure to be useful too (but we haven't used these). For winter and early spring trips a sleeping bag will prove useful. Camping gear might be of use in certain areas but is not essential for any of the sites mentioned in this guide.

Food

The best way to avoid stomach upset is to keep to well cooked food; tajines and couscous are two easily available, cheap and filling meals. In combination with bottled water and hot drinks, the chances of falling ill are slight. Fresh fruit and bread are widely available and cheap. From personal experience we would advise caution and avoid eating shellfish.

When to go

Needless to say, this very much depends on the particular species required. Spring trips were once the most popular, with pleasantly warm weather and a good all round selection of migrant and resident species, whilst of late winter trips have been more fashionable due to the publicity surrounding the few Slender-billed Curlews at Merja Zerga. Spring certainly has many attractions but it should be noted that some resident species are easier to find in numbers in autumn and winter. Most Europeans would probably find a summer (June to August) visit excessively hot. It is also worth noting that during the month-long religious festival of Ramadan, banks and shops have restricted opening times and it is not always easy to find cafes open during the day at this time.

A brief history

It is undoubtedly foolhardy to attempt a description of the recorded history of the region in a few sentences, and we urge interested readers to delve elsewhere; nevertheless the following sketches an historical framework since 1100 BC (and recalls the Woody Allen joke "I took a course in speed reading, learning to read straight down the middle of the page, and was able to read *War and Peace* in twenty minutes. It's about Russia.").

Phoenicians, Cartheginians, Romans, Vandals and even the Byzantine Empire all had at least a foothold in what is now modern Morocco, but none of these had the profound effect of the Islamic invaders of the 680s, who subjugated the Berbers, converted them to Islam and imposed Arabic as the main language. From Morocco it was but a short step across the strait and into Spain, but that of course is another story.

There followed centuries of internal wrangling and punch-ups, until European colonialist expansion in the late 19th Century began to play a part in Morocco, culminating in the establishment of so-called protectorates for both France and Spain in 1912 (this had the later unexpected spin-off of several Hollywood films where the people of the Magreb represented the Red Indians whilst the Legionnaires represented the US Cavalry).

Naturally enough, a nationalistic movement soon arose, which after a long struggle gained independence in 1956. Morocco is now a constitutional monarchy and governed by an elected parliament, although the monarchy exerts a huge influence on proceedings. The 1975 Spanish withdrawal from Western Sahara led to Moroccan involvement and conflict with the Algerian backed Polisario Front who wanted an independent Saharan state. This war has only recently been resolved, allowing the opening-up of much of the deep south to travellers.

The people

Moroccan Arabic is the official language, so learning a few well chosen words or phrases will be a great asset. A knowledge of French, as much of Morocco was formerly a colony of France, will also be useful at times. You will soon discover that the Berbers are great linguists, many knowing something of a variety of north European languages, especially Dutch, German and English. Most people are friendly but many will try to part you from your cash, offering guidance, selling souvenirs, or begging. This can be a distraction when you're trying to birdwatch but is no great problem; things are different than at home! As anywhere, it's not a good idea to leave valuables in your car overnight, or leave it unlocked. The mouth of the Oued Sous has become notorious for thievery; even if the risks are exaggerated, be watchful. Most trips have no problems. The only area which everyone agrees is very risky and best left for hardened travellers (and is not included in this guide) is the Rif. Drugs and organised crime is the problem; as a birder you don't need to go there.

A few useful words and phrases are always appreciated by the locals and, even if mispronounced, the effort rewarded, if only with amusement. Some commoner ones follow:-

Eeyeh = **yes.**
La = **no.**
La bes = **hello.**
Bslemah = **goodbye.**

Shokran = **thank you.**
Smeh lee = **excuse me.**
Bsh hal = **how much?**
Wakha = **O.K.**

Road blocks

You may be stopped by police and asked for your passport. This is most likely in the south of the country, where there is also the likelihood of a military presence (although we have experienced no problems with them). The police roadblocks can be tiresome but should present no real problems; be patient and stay calm. Although such roadblocks are not encountered in Europe they are not unusual in many countries of our acquaintance in Africa, Asia and the Americas and should present little difficulty in Morocco.

Vernacular and scientific names

There are many variations in both sets of names at present, with differences between various checklists and field guides. In this booklet we have decided to adopt those used in *The 'British Birds' List of English Names of Western Palearctic Birds (1993)*, with a few later changes, even if we find some not to our taste (e.g. Rufous-tailed Scrub-robin instead of Rufous Bush Robin or Chat for *Cercotrichas galactotes*).

Another point to consider is the definition of species as used in this list. You would have probably had to have spent the last few years in a government surplus nuclear bunker to have missed hearing at least something of the proposed changes in systematics (i.e. the concept of what constitutes a species). It is beyond the scope of this guide and the understanding of the authors to discuss this argument in any depth, but briefly, if the new method is fully adopted, subspecies will either disappear or become full species, with a potential doubling of the number of species in your field guide or handbook. Even if the current ideas of systematics prevail, there is a trend towards 'splitting' into full species rather than 'lumping' into groups of subspecies.

The implication for north-west Africa is that many endemic subspecies or groups of endemic subspecies may soon be considered as full species. For example, Jay, Magpie, Pied Flycatcher, Chaffinch and Blue Tit would be just a few of those affected. This is great news if you are a keen lister and an added reason to travel to Morocco (think of writing all those identification papers for all those new species). If, however, you are not interested in such things (or like us too thick to make much out of it), just enjoy the birds.

For anyone interested in pursuing the subject further, the paper by C.J.Hazevoet (1994) discusses the new ideas in systematics, whilst the articles by George Sangster (1996a, 1996b) presents his arguments for splitting Blue Tit into up to six species and Houbara Bustard into two (see bibliography). If this leaves you none the wiser, at least then you will be better informed.

Bibliography

The following bibliography includes a selection of books and guides which we consider helpful and worth taking on your trip if space permits. It also includes a number of papers mentioned in the text which might prove useful references. Of course there are many other works such as *BWP*, the published volumes of *Birds of Africa* and the species group guides from *Pica Press* and *Helm/A&C Black* which will prove invaluable reference before and after your trip. Various items of interest concerning Morocco appear in the monthly magazines *British Birds, Birdwatch* and *Birding World*, and we also unreservedly recommend the bi-monthly *Dutch Birding* as essential reading.

ANON. (1993). *The 'British Birds' List of English Names of Western Palearctic Birds*. Blunham.

CHANTLER, P. (1993). Identification of Western Palearctic Swifts. *Dutch Birding* 15:97-135.

ELLINGHAM, M. & McVEIGH, S. *The rough guide to Morocco*. London.

ETCHÉCOPAR, R.D. & HUE, F. (1967). *The Birds of North Africa*. Edinburgh.

FINLAYSON, C. (1992). *Birds of the Strait of Gibraltar*. London.

HARRIS, A., SHIRIHAI, H. & CHRISTIE, D.A. (1996). *The Macmillan Birder's Guide to European and Middle Eastern Birds* . London.

HAZEVOET, C.J. (1996). Species concepts and systematics. *Dutch Birding* 16:111-116.

HEINZEL, H., FITTER, R. & PARSLOW, J. (1996). *Collins Pocket Guide. Birds of Britain & Europe with North Africa & the Middle East*. London.

HOLLOM, P., PORTER, R., CHRISTENSEN, S. & WILLIS, R. (1988). *Birds of the Middle East and North Africa*. Calton.

JONSSON, L. (1992). *Birds of Europe*. London.

SANGSTER, G. (1996a). Species limits in the Blue Tit complex: new evidence from play-back studies. *Dutch Birding* 18:85-88.

SANGSTER, G. (1996b). Taxonomy of Houbara and Macqueen's Bustards and the neglect of intraspecific diversity. *Dutch Birding* 18:248-256.

ULLMAN, M. (1994). Crested and Thekla Larks in Morocco. *Dutch Birding* 16:19-20.

VAN DEN BURG, A.B. (1988). Identification of Slender-billed Curlew and its occurrence in the winter of 1987-88. *Dutch Birding* 10:45-53

VAN DEN BURG, A.B. (1990). Habitat of Slender-billed Curlews in Morocco. *British Birds* 83:1-7.

WALTER, H. (1979). *Eleonora's Falcon*. Chicago.

Key to Maps

═══	Roads (Sketches)	▓	Town Fill
～	Roads (Main Map)	▒	Cultivation
──	Coastline	☐	Water
– – ⇁	Tracks	☐	Building
▬▬▬	Railway	⊡	Hotel/Cafe/Auberge
–·–·–	International Bdy	♣	Trees
⊥⊤⊥	ET Line	🦅	Bird Site
～	Rivers	Λ	Camp Site
⬬	Lakes	✈	Airport
▨	Mountains	⊙	Village/Town
+ + +	Telegraph Poles	⚑	Mile Post
⌢	Bridges	●	Text Site
⬭	Sand Dunes	•	Town

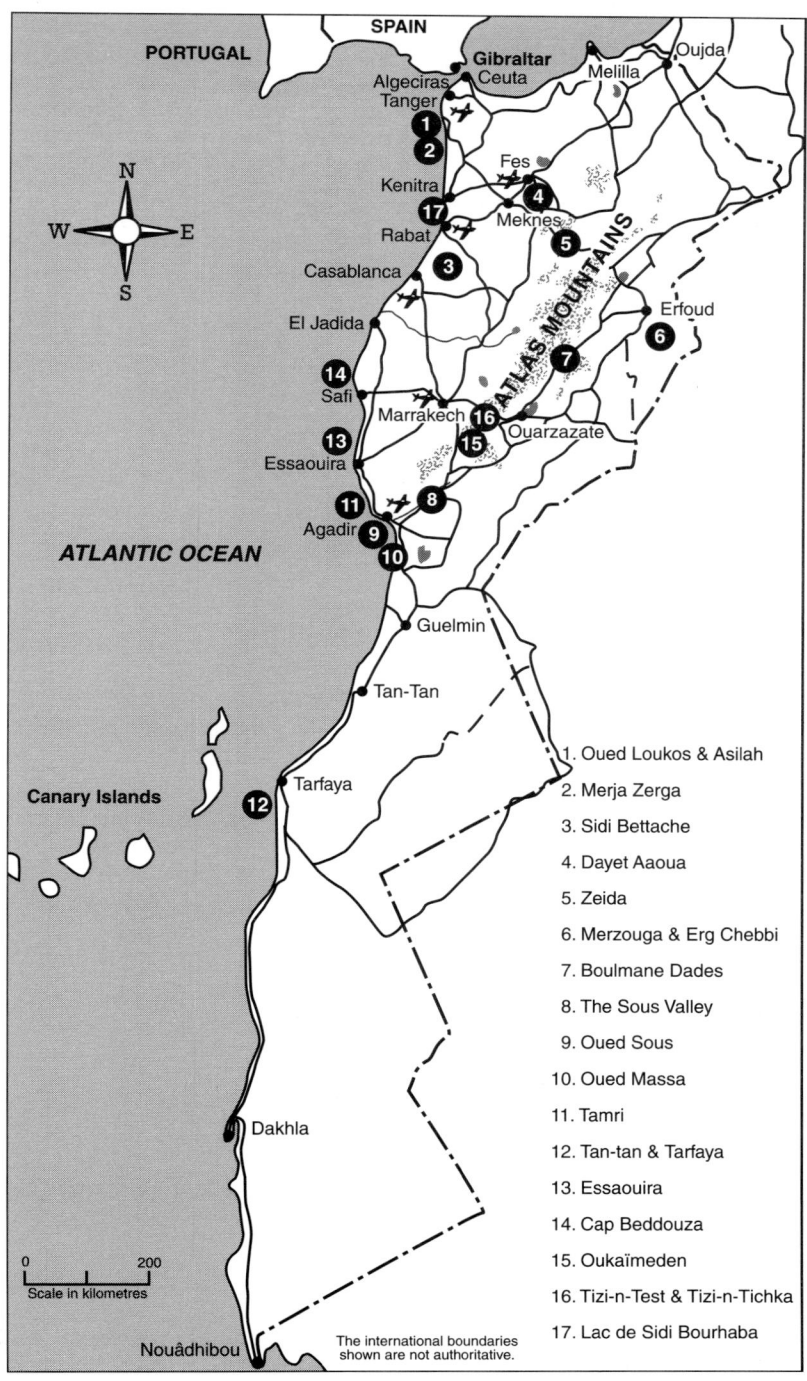

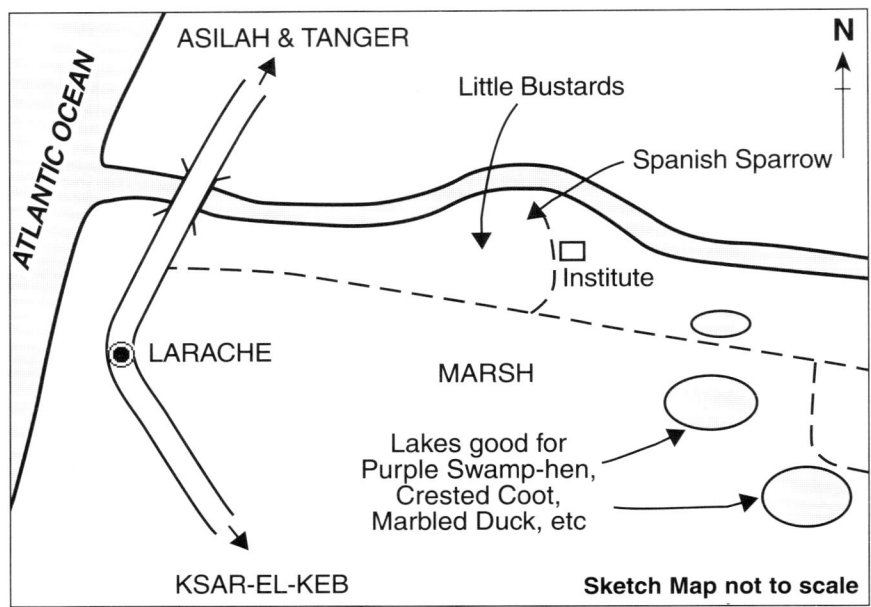
Map 1. Oued Loukos.

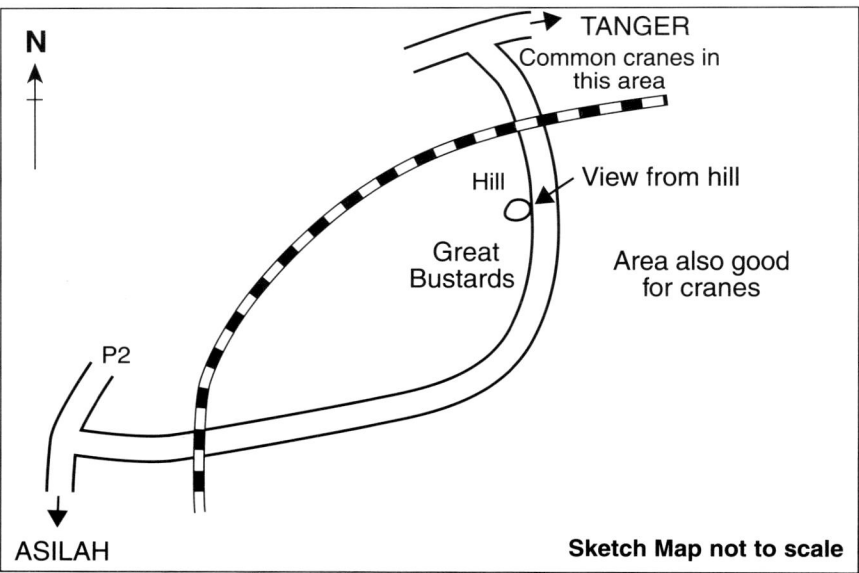
Map 1a. Oued Loukos.

No. 1 Oued Loukos & Asilah

Both these sites are conveniently close to Tanger. Larache, recently a disappointment to some, is about 88 kms south of the city. Purple Swamp-hen, Crested Coot, Squacco Heron and a variety of wildfowl, including Marbled and Ferruginous Ducks, and sometimes Red-

Plate 1. *Mouth of the Oued Massa.* Mike Combridge

Plate 2. *Stream in the High Atlas.* Mike Combridge

Plate 3. *Erg Chebbi.* Mike Combridge

Plate 4. *Near Er-Rachida.* Mike Combridge

crested Pochard, have all been encountered here. Moustached Warbler and Spanish Sparrow are among the more interesting passerines possible at this site, and Penduline Tit has been seen here too. Little Bustards have been regularly reported but are often difficult to see, so don't give up too easily if they are not immediately apparent. Occasional vagrants such as Ring-billed Gull have also been recorded.

Asilah, (see map 1a), on the P2 between Larache and Tanger, is known as a good site to observe some of the small Moroccan population of Great Bustards. These are best viewed from the minor road as indicated on the sketch map. They can be rather distant, so a telescope is an essential item here.

Don't forget that in spring and autumn the Tanger peninsula is a great place to observe migration. To the west of the city Cap Spartel provides an obvious watchpoint, whilst to the east Cap Malabata and Punta Ceres are worthy of attention. The first two named are generally considered best in easterly winds, whilst the latter is recommended in westerlies. For full details of the migration hereabouts, read *Birds of the Strait of Gibraltar* by Clive Finlayson (1992) for a mainly Spanish perspective.

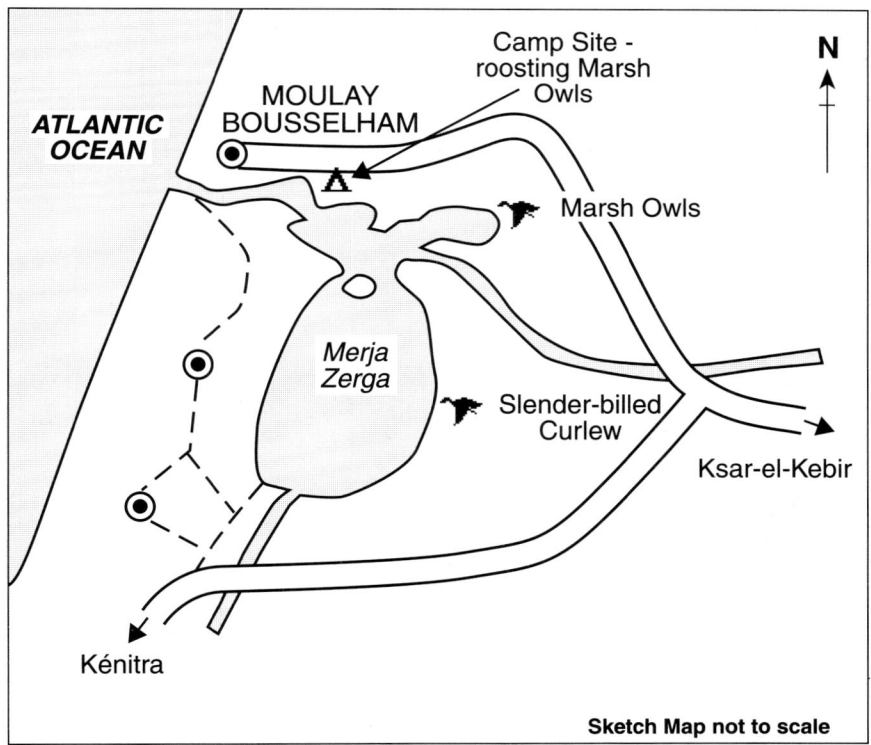

Map 2. Merja Zerga.

No. 2 Merja Zerga

For several winters this area was most famous as the only widely known stake-out for wintering Slender-billed Curlew, arguably the species responsible for returning Morocco to fashion with the birding fraternity (e.g. van den Burg 1988, 1990). However, recent winters have proved frustrating for ornithological tourists intent on this species and, sadly, it may well now be yet another former locality of this once common but now highly endangered wader.

Despite the probable demise of the sought-after curlews, this remains a very fine place to birdwatch, with, in winter, impressive numbers and a wide range of species. Another key species, Marsh Owl, can be found roosting in the campsite and elsewhere around the lake; not surprisingly the owls can also be observed hunting at dusk. Also in winter, the area is extremely good for large numbers of ducks (especially Eurasian Wigeon) and waders (especially Dunlin and Black-tailed Godwit). Other possibilities here include Greater Flamingo (Camargue ringed individuals have been recorded here), Eurasian Spoonbill, Ruddy Shelduck, White Stork, Common Crane and Calandra Lark.

The site is less well-known to European-based birdwatchers in summer, but Montagu's Harrier, Collared Pratincole and Red-necked Nightjar are amongst the species of interest likely to be recorded in that season. Both spring and autumn can also be interesting, with migrants such as Whiskered Tern recorded. As elsewhere on the Moroccan coastline, vagrants are always a possibility, with, for example, Ring-billed Gull from the Americas and Allen's Gallinule from sub-Saharan Africa noted.

No. 3 Sidi Bettache

The forest between Sidi Bettache and Sidi Yahia is the famous site for Double-spurred Francolin which, although widespread in tropical Africa, is represented in Morocco by the endemic and threatened race *ayesha*. Early mornings are considered best for views of this gamebird, and there is a good chance of seeing other interesting species such as Barbary Partridge, Black-shouldered Kite and Black-crowned Tchagra.

The area is a Royal hunting preserve, so it will come as no surprise that birdwatchers have been turned away and discouraged here, and that access is more restricted now than in the past. Be sensible and keep to the road! (See map page 17).

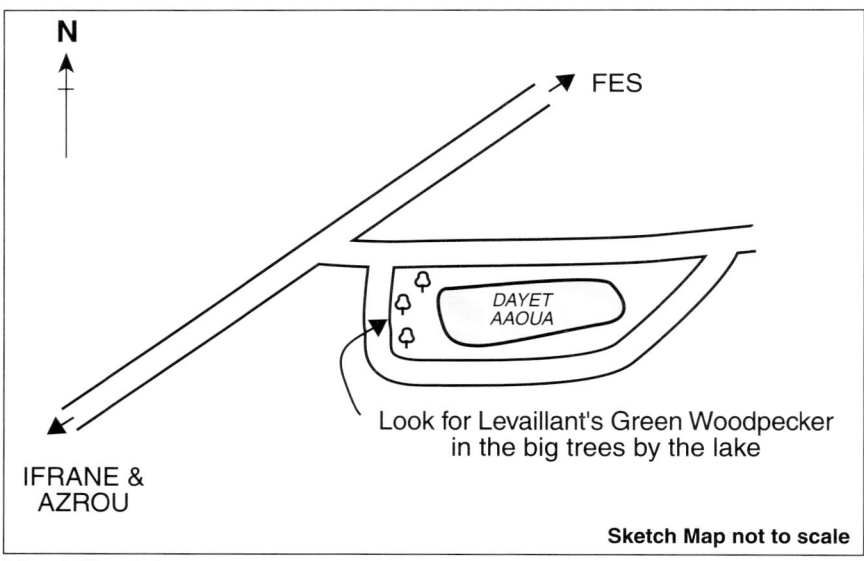

Map 4. Dayet Aaoua.

No. 4 Dayet Aaoua

The Ifrane area is known for its beautiful woods and attractive small lakes. The Dayet Aaoua, close to the main Fes to Azrou road, is as convenient a spot as any to search for the endemic Levaillant's Green Woodpecker. Although widespread in the woods, they

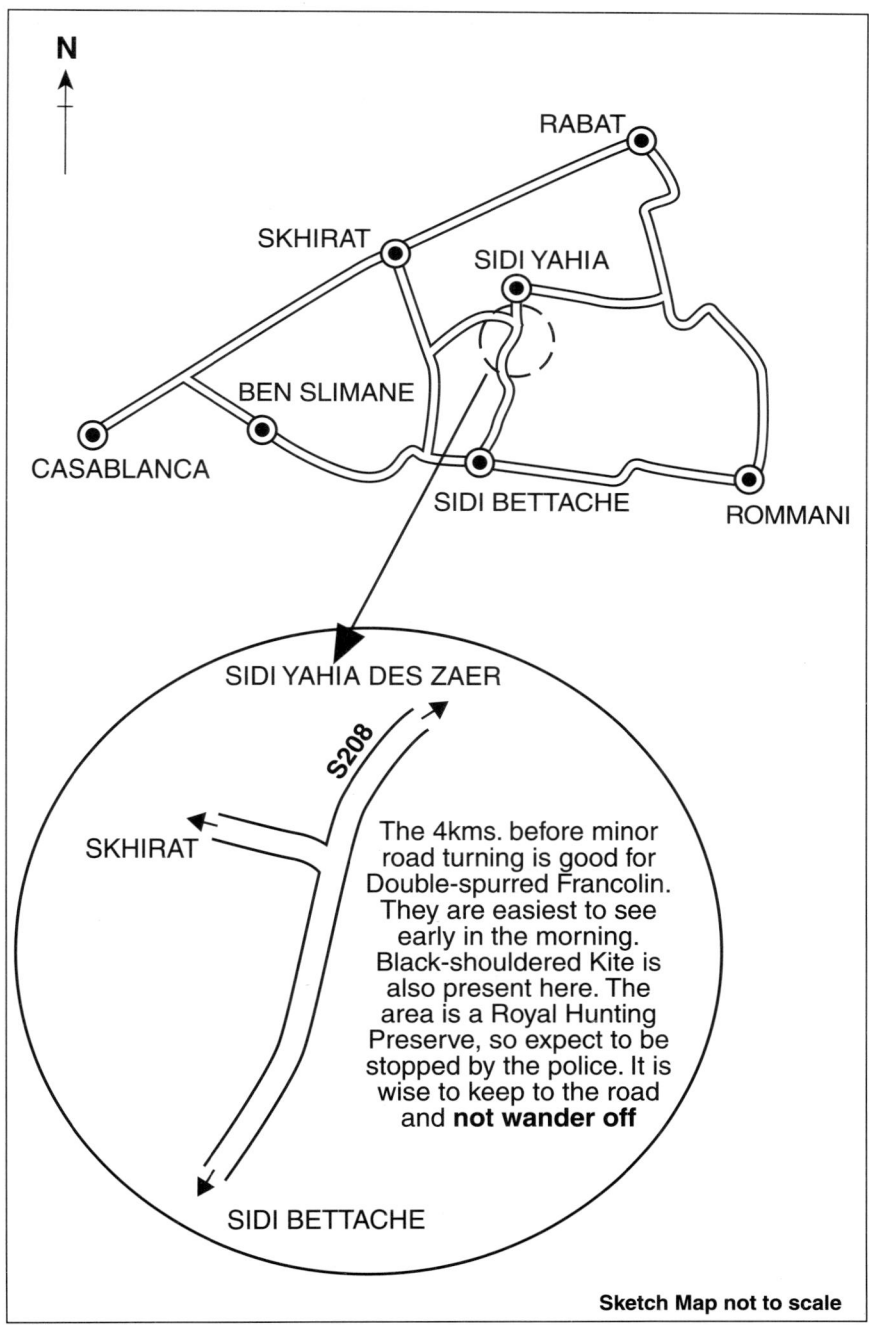

Map 3. Sidi Bettache.

seem especially easy here: most who look see them! If time permits, it may well be worth exploring the other lakes and surrounding woodland in the area between Ifrane and the P20; in the appropriate habitat and season a good range of species can be found, including Crested Coot, Little Bittern, Long-legged Buzzard, Short-toed and Booted Eagles, Wood Lark, Olivaceous, Melodious and Western Bonelli's Warblers, and Cirl Bunting. Note too that many of the familiar European birds are represented by unfamiliar races; "Seebohm's" Wheatear and *speculigera* Pied Flycatchers being just two examples.

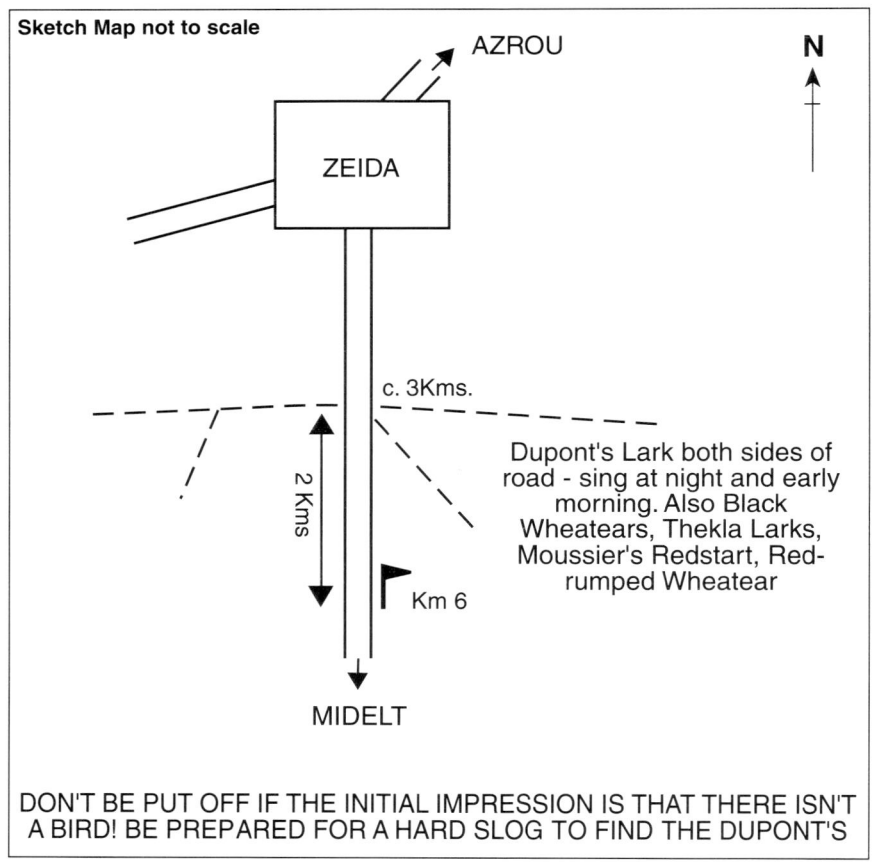

Map 5. Zeida.

No. 5 Zeida

This is the best known site in Morocco for that pimpernel of the steppe, Dupont's Lark. Although Dupont's obviously occurs elsewhere, Zeida provides a convenient stake-out on the way to the riches of the south.

As hinted at above, this lark is notorious for being exceedingly elusive, so, apart from patience, a good tactic might be to arrive before dawn, when they can be heard singing; at least you then know that they are there, even if you still can't see them! At certain times this area can initially seem totally birdless, but a little persistence should be rewarded with other species including Thekla Lark, Moussier's Redstart and Black and Red-rumped Wheatears.

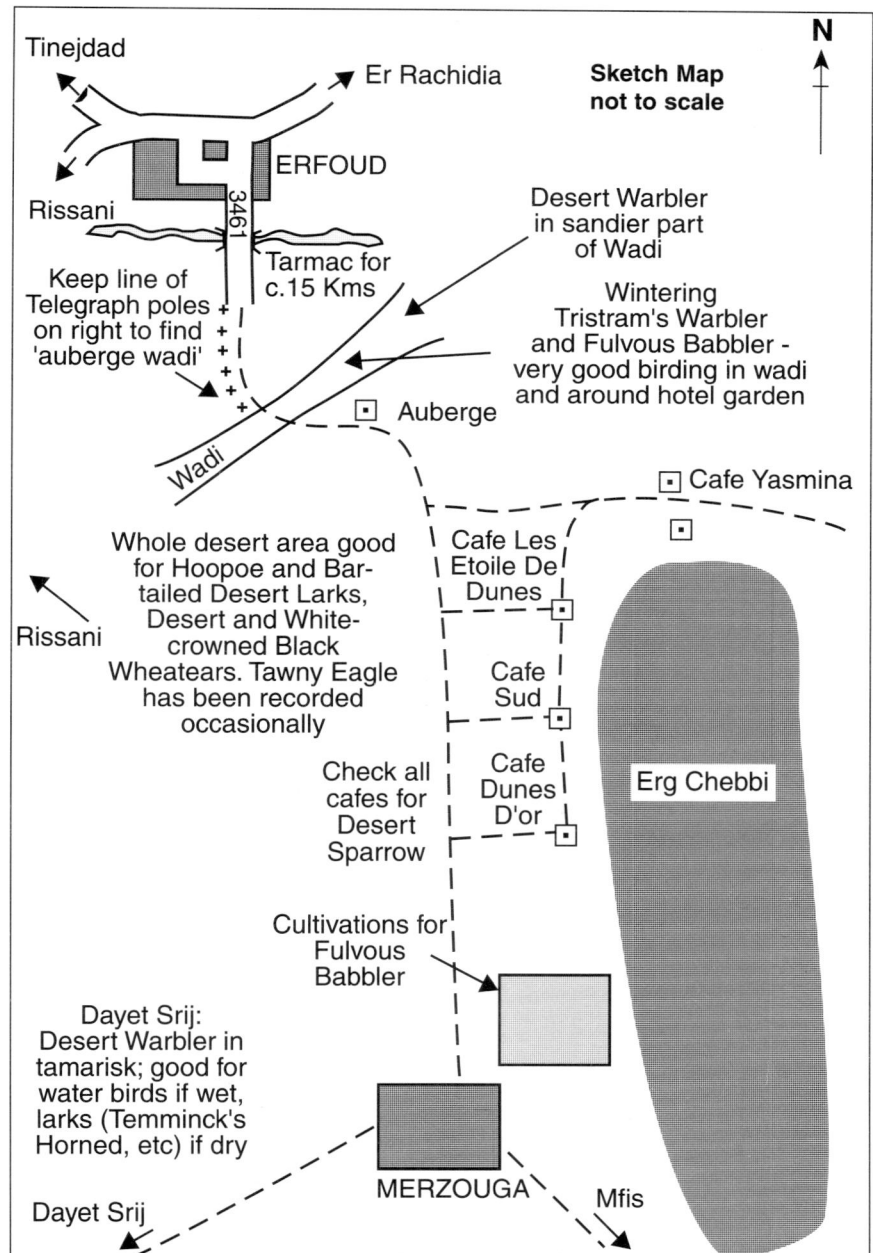

Map 6. Merzouga & The Erg Chebbi.

No. 6 Merzouga & The Erg Chebbi

Situated in the south-east of the country, hard by the Algerian border in the region known as the Tafilat, this is a taste of the Sahara. Follow the 3461 out of Erfoud. After 15 kms or so the tarmac disappears but, contrary to what you may have been told in Erfoud by the local hustlers, no guide is needed to find the Erg Chebbi, the largest sand dune in Morocco. Avoiding anyone who tries to stop you to tell you otherwise, follow the unmade tracks, keeping the line of telegraph poles on your right at all times; it should then be impossible to get lost. Some care will be needed to avoid areas of soft sand both on the way to and on excursions from Merzouga. It is all too easy to get bogged-down in a saloon car; whilst it should be easy to find a local with a four wheeled drive vehicle to pull you out, it will cost you dear!

By following the telegraph poles, you will eventually come to a wadi, beyond which is a well appointed and fairly expensive hotel; if you are going to indulge in comfort at some stage of your trip, is there a better spot to do so? The gardens of the hotel often host Fulvous Babbler and are a good place to look for migrants. The wadi, too, holds migrants in the appropriate season and, in winter, Tristram's Warbler. It is well worth walking to where the wadi opens up and becomes sandier, as Desert Warbler has been noted there. Other species recorded include Lanner Falcon, Marsh Harrier, Cream-coloured Courser, Mourning and Desert Wheatears, Bar-tailed Desert and Hoopoe Larks, and Trumpeter Finch. Mornings are probably the most productive time to birdwatch in the wadi.

The track continues past the auberge towards Merzouga, with ill defined (but signposted) tracks striking off towards the cafes on the periphery of the Erg Chebbi. This large sand dune is a really atmospheric place, and it is possible to stay cheaply at the cafes. The number one attraction for birdwatchers at the cafes are of course Desert Sparrows, which breed nearby in the Erg. The sparrows can usually be found at one or more of the cafes, around the buildings themselves and their associated wells and camel feeders. The largest numbers are present around the cafes in winter. It may be possible to find a guide to take you to the breeding site in the Erg, although it is a tough walk.

Both Brown-necked and Common Ravens are hereabouts, and provide an interesting identification challenge. The area is also good for wintering Tristram's and Desert Warblers (try the scrub by the Dayet Srij), and Fulvous Babbler. The Dayet Srij is a seasonal lake, which, although still worth scrub bashing for passerines if dry, is obviously more productive with at least some water. If wet, a variety of species such as Greater Flamingo, Common Coot, Ruddy Shelduck, Common Pochard, Northern Pintail, Black-winged Stilt and a range of other wildfowl and waders are possible. Both Kittlitz's Plover and Egyptian Courser have been recorded as vagrants here.

Apart from those species mentioned above, Black-bellied and Crowned Sandgrouse, Stone Curlew, Desert and Lesser Short-toed Larks, White-crowned Black Wheatear, Spectacled and Streaked Scrub Warblers are all likely in the desert. Isabelline Wheatear has been recorded as a vagrant on more than one occasion in winter. There is also a better chance of finding Spotted Sandgrouse here than at the Tagdilt track.

A species well worth looking for is Egyptian Nightjar. As nightjars often sit on roads at night, patrolling the track either side of the auberge is worth a try; they have been seen by car headlights in this way.

The area was also well known for both Houbara and Arabian Bustards, although as is also well known, these birds have suffered from intense hunting pressure from Arab falconers in the winter months.

It has been very unlikely to see Arabian Bustard for some time now, with Houbara regarded the more realistic target. However, even these have become exceedingly difficult to find in recent winters, and it may well prove that they have been hunted-out. That said, you may still care to hire a Landrover (we certainly would not recommend the use of a saloon car in the likely areas) and guide to search for Houbaras. There will be no shortage of volunteers to guide you; the problem will be choosing the right one! Ask around the cafes and hope you choose well. Both bustards (more especially Houbara) were often seen in the area around Mfis, and to the south-west of Rissani. Good luck!

Tristram's and Desert Warblers

No. 7 Boulmane Dades

This town provides a good base to explore the stony desert towards Tagdilt (regarded by some as the highlight of a Moroccan birding tour) and the nearby Gorges du Dades. The Gorges du Todra near Tinehir can also be visited if time permits. The Tagdilt Track area is excellent for larks: Thick-billed and Temminck's Horned can both be found easily from autumn through to spring, whilst Short-toed and Lesser Short-toed can be studied close at hand. Bar-tailed Desert and Hoopoe Lark are here too, but in lesser numbers than in the Merzouga area. The latter's nest is surprisingly easy to find, sometimes being placed in the top of a bush! The elusive Dupont's Lark has recently been discovered here but remains, as always, far from a certainty.

It is also a good area to connect with sandgrouse, with Pin-tailed, Black-bellied, Crowned and, perhaps, Spotted all possible, although their relative abundance varies with the season and between years; it would be unlucky, however, not to find at least one of the first three species in the area, with Black-bellied the most likely. Red-rumped Wheatears are very common here, and Long-legged Buzzard, Lanner Falcon, Cream-coloured Courser, Spectacled Warbler and Trumpeter Finch are all regular. Look out, too, for the small desert race of Eagle Owl around the wadis at dusk. Common Raven is often seen here, and Brown-necked has been reported too; so careful study is required for safe identification.

This site was formerly very much a certainty for Houbara Bustard. However, in the 1990s they have increasingly fallen foul of Arab falconers (much to the disgust of many of the Berber locals) and can no longer be guaranteed. If you do find any, please do not push them too hard for closer views.

The best way to work the area is to steadily drive the desert tracks, frequently stopping and scanning the surroundings, with occasional forays on foot along the wadi edges. By using the car as a hide, good views and photographic opportunities will be obtained of the

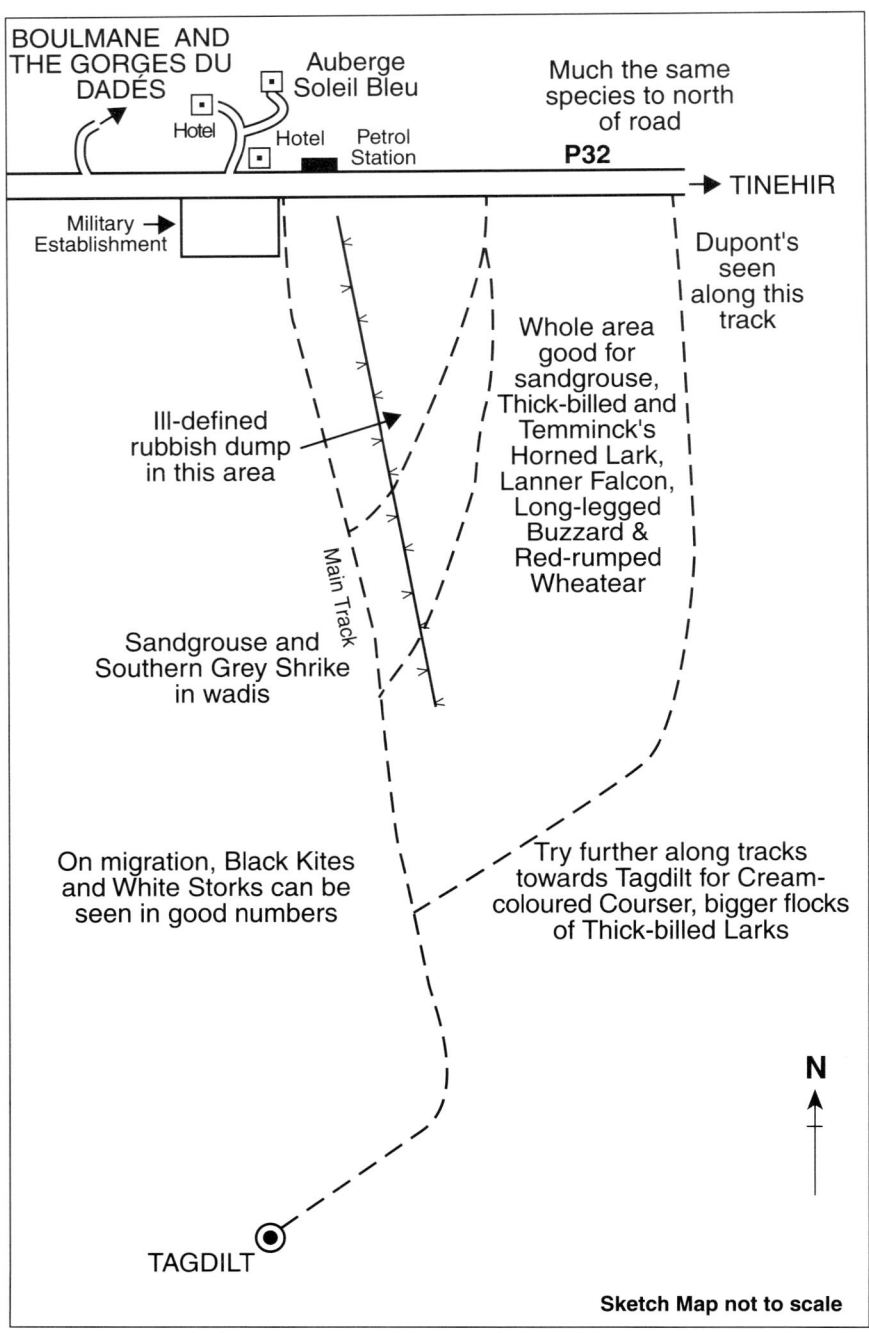

Map 7. Boulmane Dades

Desert Wheatear

larks, sandgrouse and perhaps even Houbara.

The nearby Gorges du Dades is worth at least a half day of exploration. Black Wheatear is common here, as are Crag Martins and Common Raven. The ubiquitous Moussier's Redstart and the inevitable House Bunting will be seen, andTristram's Warblers, Rock Sparrows and Rock Buntings may be found. Crimson-winged Finch is certainly present in winter and worth seeking out if you are not going to Oukaïmeden. The highly scenic Gorges du Todra holds similar species to the Gorges du Dades and is pretty touristy, but is still worth a visit if time permits.

If you are staying in Boulmane, the Auberge Soleil Bleu is a very good place to stay. It boasts a logbook of bird sightings, the food is very good and, being situated to the east of the town, it is highly convenient for the desert. In winter and early spring the rooms often seem colder than outside, so a sleeping bag is recommended. On request, it is possible to use the piping hot showers; a welcome change from the cold or lukewarm showers elsewhere! In winter this high and stony desert can be bitterly cold with snow, so go prepared with warm clothing.

Just over a 100 kms west of Boulmane lies the garrison town of Ouarzazate, through which most birders at some stage pass. The corner of the large reservoir here is a good spot to see Ruddy Shelduck, and there is usually a range of other wildfowl, waders and hirundines here too. Black Kites roost in the trees on the lake edge. The rubbish dump to the east of the town is also a very good place for Black Kites, especially at migration times when hundreds can be present. Exploration of likely-looking wadis either side of the town is often rewarding for various wheatears (including Mourning), Trumpeter Finch, Spanish Sparrow and migrants.

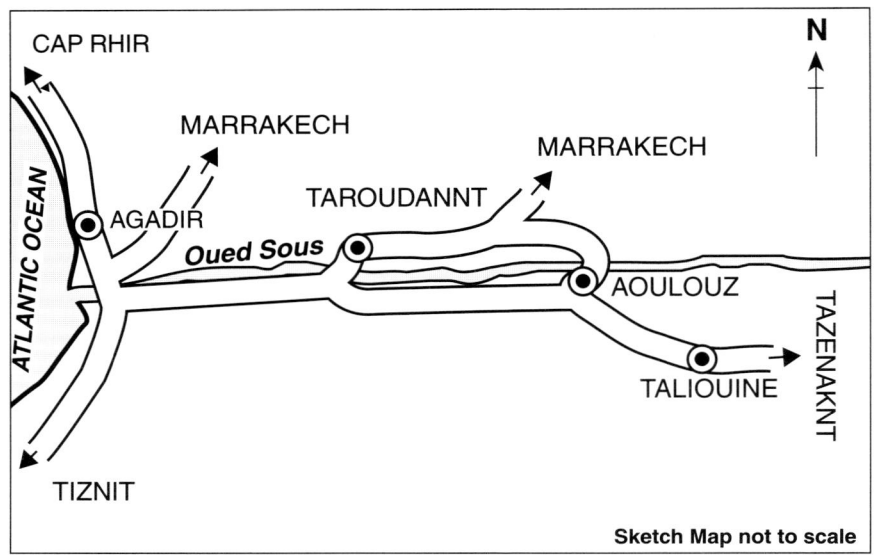

Map 8/9. Valley of the Sous.

No. 8 The Sous Valley

The valley of the Oued Sous holds a unique habitat, Argana woodland, and is the only Palearctic home of the Dark Chanting Goshawk, a charismatic raptor more widely distributed south of the Sahara. The area between Aoulouz (an old site for Bald Ibis) and Taroudannt has been the best area in recent times for publicised sightings of this raptor. The village of Igoudar (reached by a track 2 kms west of Oled Berhil) is a recent and well-known site for this species. Many pilgrims have, however, been disappointed, but it may still be worth a look. Other species hereabouts include Black-shouldered Kite, Bonelli's and Tawny Eagles, Spanish Sparrow, Black-crowned Tchagra, Moussier's Redstart and Cirl Bunting. If this site fails for the goshawk, then (time permitting) it is probably worthwhile exploring for other suitable watchpoints in this part of the valley; even if this draws a blank too, other interesting raptors may well be in evidence.

Apart from those species mentioned above, Lanner and Barbary Falcons, Red-necked Nightjar, Rufous-tailed Scrub-robin and even White-rumped Swift have been recorded from the Aoulouz to Taroudannt area. The wadi just to the west of Taroudannt is a known site for Red-necked Nightjar, but of course they are much more widespread than this and can be found elsewhere in suitable habitat. All the wadis are worth checking for migrants in the appropriate seasons.

Taliouine, to the east of Aoulouz, has Rock Sparrows around the ruined Casbah, whilst on the higher ground further east the mysterious Dupont's Lark has been seen. The auberge in Taliouine, close to the old Casbah, is a splendid place to stay, with ample supplies of good food and an eccentric cook.

No. 9 The Mouth of the Oued Sous

This excellent area, also the site of a Royal Palace, is 7 kms south of Agadir, and is thus highly convenient for anyone staying at this popular resort. It can be easily reached by road (a track from Inezgane follows the northern side of the wadi) or by walking along the shore from Agadir.

Greater Flamingo, Audouin's Gull, Ruddy Shelduck in winter, Barbary Partridge,

Black-crowned Tchagra, Moussier's Redstart and Plain Martin (of the small, pale race *mauritanica*) are amongst those species likely to be seen here. It also a good locality for Slender-billed Gull, and Red-necked Nightjar can be encountered in the vicinity of the Royal Palace at dusk.

Scarcer species such as Lesser Crested and Royal Terns have been recorded and, being so close to Agadir and thus comparatively well-watched, it has an impressive list of rarities. These include Lesser Flamingo, Spotted Sandpiper, Lesser Yellowlegs, Semi-palmated Sandpiper and, best of all so far, the Western Palearctic's first reported (but actually second) Great Knot.

The only negative point to report at present is that this area, especially the south side of the wadi, has gained a bad reputation for thievery of late. Violence has sometimes been used, so take care!

Agadir itself boasts Spotless Starlings, and Glaucous Gull has been recorded in the harbour, which is undoubtedly worth checking if time permits.

Bald Ibis

No. 10 Oued Massa

This renowned site is well worth a day or two of anyone's Moroccan birdwatching tour. There is still a fair chance of Bald Ibis here (try watching at dusk for birds flighting along the coast), and a good selection of species of interest to the north European birder, including Plain Martin.

The main feature of the site is the area between the small village and the wadi mouth. A good range of ducks (Marbled Duck regularly, and Ruddy Shelduck, Red-crested Pochard and Ferruginous Duck more rarely) and other species such as Greater Flamingo, egrets, Spoonbill and Glossy Ibis could be present and, in winter, Common Crane and Bluethroat.

Take time to search the scrub for Black-crowned Tchagra (often easier to hear than see) and Barbary Partridge. It can be pretty good for migrant passerines in the appropriate season, and, perhaps surprisingly, Richard's Pipit has been regularly noted in winter.

Around the wadi mouth and along the beach is good for waders, including Kentish Plover, and gulls and terns. Audouin's and Yellow-legged Gulls should be found here, and there is always a chance of Slender-billed Gull and Caspian Tern as well. Attempts at seawatching mostly produce Northern Gannet and Arctic and Great Skuas, but Cory's and Mediterranean Shearwaters, Bulwer's Petrel and even Wilson's Storm-petrel have been seen. A 'soft-plumaged petrel' was claimed here in March 1995. Do not forget to check any muddy areas at the wadi edge for crakes.

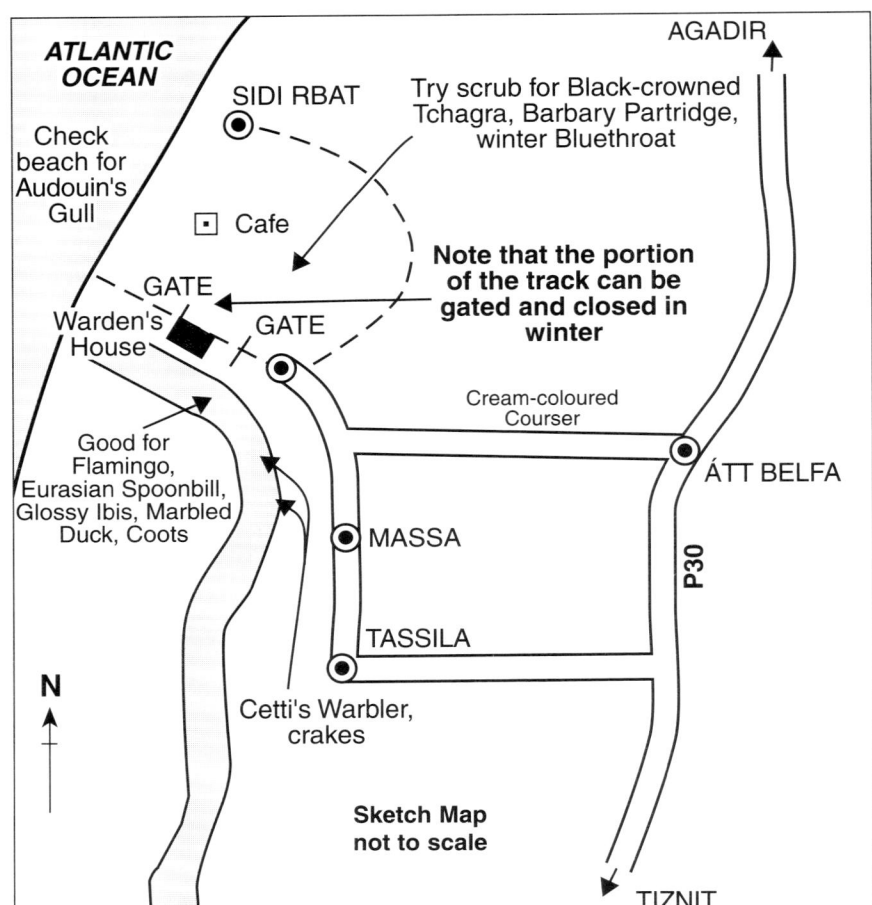

Map 10. Oued Massa.

As this site is relatively well watched, a fair number of scarce and rare species have been recorded over the years, including Royal and Lesser Crested Terns, Laughing Gull, Slender-billed Curlew (once more regular) and Long-billed Dowitcher. No doubt close and regular observation would reveal this as a prime site for Nearctic and Afrotropical vagrants.

The arid areas surrounding the Oued Massa hold dry country species including Stone Curlew, sandgrouse and Cream-coloured Courser. Tawny Eagle has also been regularly recorded in the area.

Food and simple accommodation is available behind the beach at nearby Sidi Rbat, although it is all too easy to get bogged down in the sand if driving from the wadi mouth. Whether you stay here or in Agadir, this really is a site not to be missed.

No. 11 Tamri

About an hours drive north from the town of Agadir will bring you to Tamri, one of the most reliable and accessible sites for the rapidly declining Bald Ibis. Even if the ibis are not immediately apparent, you can be amused by the swarms of locals offering to show

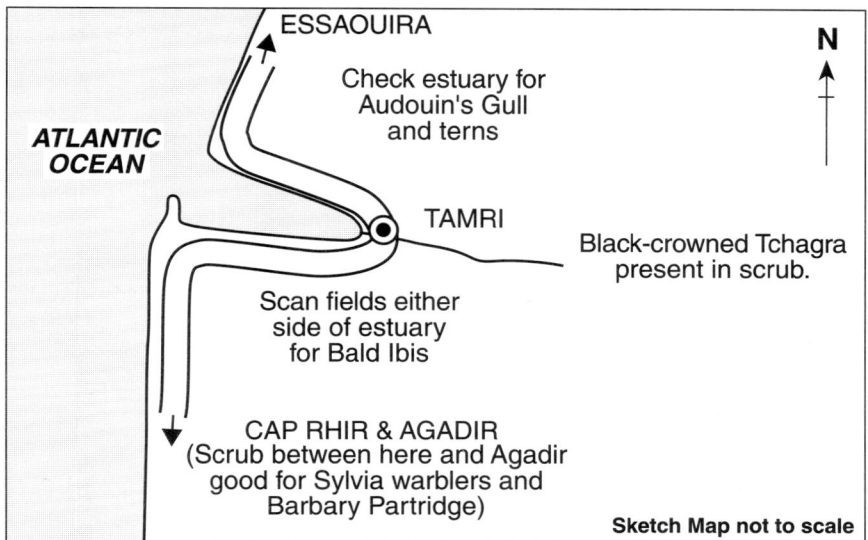

Map 11. Tamri.

you this species – for a fee, of course! Most of these guides claim any largish bird, gulls, corvids etc as Bald Ibis, which gives you some idea of their usefulness! They are probably better avoided. The ibis can be located on the cliffs, feeding just inland, and on the estuary itself. Some patient searching may be required both to the north and to the south of the estuary.

Other birds hereabouts include Audouin's Gull, terns, egrets, Spoonbill and Barbary Falcon. The scrub is worth a look for migrants, Barbary Partridge and Black-crowned Tchagra.

If you enjoy seawatching, Cap Rhir, between Agadir and Tamri, provides a useful vantage point. As always, Northern Gannets and the commoner skuas and "tubenoses" are most likely, but rarer species such as Madeiran Storm-petrel have been seen. Moussier's Redstart and Tawny Pipits are just two of the passerines to be found here, whilst a walk north from the lighthouse offers yet another chance of Bald Ibis. Some birders have been plagued by children here, who have the delightful habit of throwing stones!

No. 12 Guelmin, Tan-Tan, Tarfaya & Dakhla

For those based in Agadir who do not intend to visit the Tagdilt track and Merzouga, an excursion between Guelmin and Tan-Tan is worthwhile for desert species. For the adventurous birder, a trip to Tarfaya and beyond to the recently accessible Dakhla adds a pioneering edge to a Moroccan tour.

Guelmin lies about 190 kms to the south of Agadir, and it is between here and Tan-Tan, a further 125 kms south, that good areas for desert species can be found. If you are not intent on travelling to Tan-Tan, then a trip to about 50 kms south of Guelmin should produce Black-bellied Sandgrouse, Thekla, Hoopoe and Bar-tailed Desert Larks, Red-rumped and Desert Wheatears, Spanish Sparrow and Southern Grey Shrike. This area may well be better in winter, when Tawny Eagles, Fulvous Babblers and Desert and Streaked Scrub Warblers can all be found. The area is easily worked from the road and by occasionally driving a short distance along the unmade tracks.

Beyond Tan-Tan, the road follows the coast to Tarfaya, where Plain Swift has reliably been reported in winter and seawatching could well be interesting in the right conditions. Past Tarfaya the road eventually leads into the former Spanish Sahara and on to the town of Dakhla, the new birding frontier of Morocco.

Recent winter birding trips to Dakhla have discovered good numbers of Royal Terns, as well as Lesser Crested and Caspian Terns. It is also an excellent area for Spotted Sandgrouse and may well prove to be the best area left in Morocco for Houbara Bustard. Migration periods could prove very interesting as well, and it seems well positioned for vagrants from further south. Although now open to tourists, there is still an obvious military and police presence here. Be prepared for frequent road blocks between Guelmin and Dakhla. The Dakhla area is apparently still sown with landmines, so clearly a large degree of caution is required. It is probably advisable to concentrate on the bay at Dakhla and, if you must wander in the nearby desert, stick to obviously well-used tracks. It is also worth noting that tourists are not allowed to enter Mauritania from Morocco, and it is not unlikely that your passport will be held by the police to ensure that you don't!

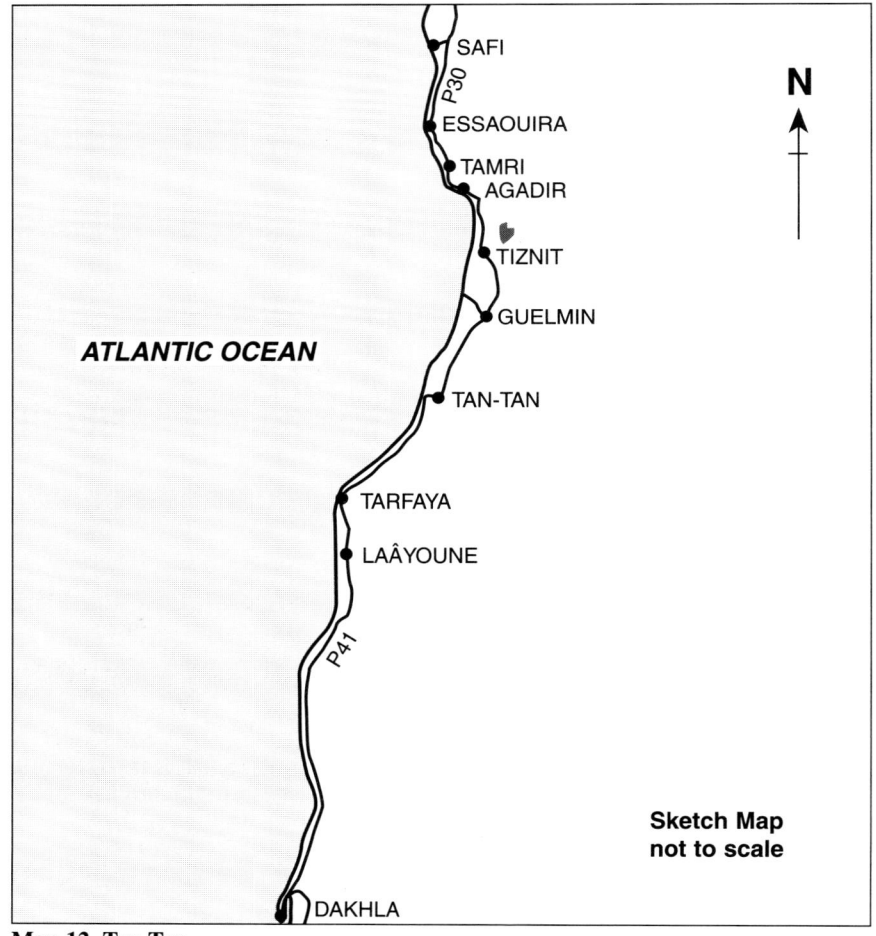

Map 12. Tan Tan

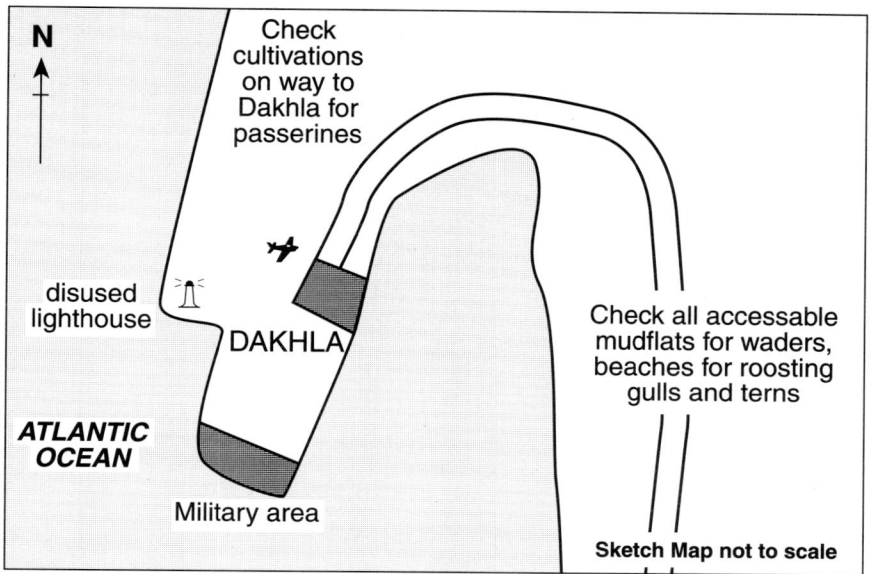

Map 12a. Dakhla.

No. 13 Essaouira

Yes folks, it's inevitable that any birdwatching guide to Morocco has got to mention the Ille de Mogador, famous for its breeding Eleonora's Falcons, even if nowadays these most spectacular raptors aren't the main reason for most birders Moroccan visit.

However, it's a pleasant and likable enough spot, with plenty of accommodation, and Plain Martins, House Buntings, Moussier's Redstarts and Spotless Starlings frequent the area. As always in Morocco, it is well worth checking through the gulls: in late January 1995 a Glaucous-winged Gull was discovered here, a quite outstanding and surprising record (see *Dutch Birding* 17:77 for a photograph of this individual).

Bald Ibis & Morroco Cormorant

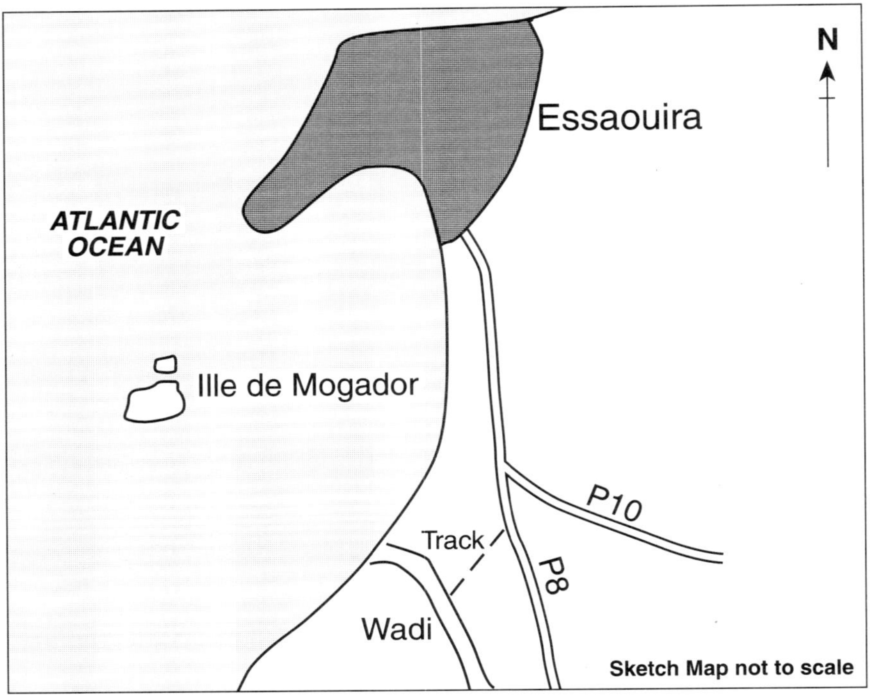

Map 13. Essaouira.

Although the Ille de Mogador can be observed from the seafront at Essaouira, it is rather distant, and much better views can be obtained of the Eleonora's as they hunt the wadi to the south of the town. This wadi is also the best area for observing Plain Martin.

If you are here to see Eleonora's Falcon, remember that they are late migrants, not arriving before the end of April, and will be gone by the end of October. A really marvellous species; read Harmut Walter's book (1979) for a first class account of it's life history.

Desert Warbler

Plate 5. North side of the Atlas.   Mike Combridge

Plate 6. Road to Zagora.   Mike Combridge

Plate 7. *Gorges Du Todra.* Mike Combridge

Plate 8. *Cafe Yasmina at the Erg Chebbi.* Mike Combridge

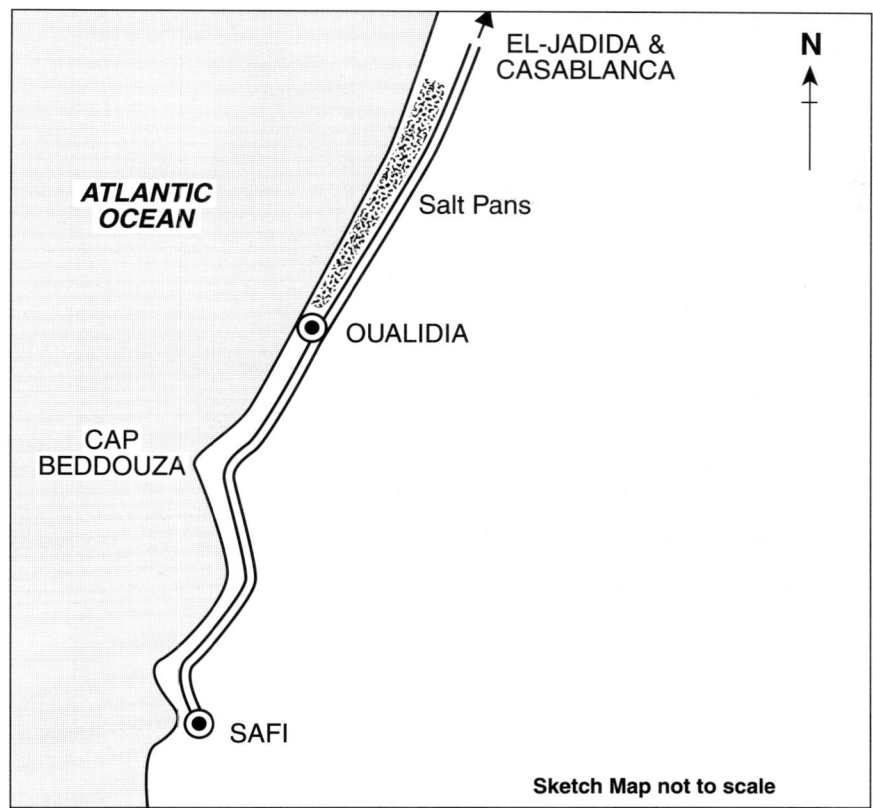

Map 14. Cap Beddouza.

No. 14 Cap Beddouza & Oualida Salt Pans

A glance at a map of coastal Morocco reveals Cap Beddouza, just to the north of Safi, as a promising seawatch point, and certainly there are enough casual records to suggest that this feeling is justified. Apart from the usual Northern Gannets, a wide range of seabirds including Grey Phalaropes, and Great, Pomarine and Arctic Skuas have been reported, as have various storm-petrels (including Madeiran) and shearwaters (including Little). Well worth a look if the conditions seem suitable; who knows what the keen seawatcher might observe?

To the north of Cap Beddouza is Oualida, beyond which lie some 40 kms of salt pans. Not surprisingly these have proved good for birds and boast an extensive list, which include various herons, Greater Flamingo, Eurasian Spoonbill, Marbled Duck and a range of waders including Collared Pratincole. Passerines such as Bluethroat have been recorded, and a fair number of rarities too, including Slender-billed Curlew and Blue-winged Teal.

If you are travelling between Safi and Marrakech the Sebka Zima, an area of salt pans to the west of Chemaïa, are worthy of investigation; Greater Flamingos and an array of waders are possible.

No. 15 Oukaïmeden

Lying some 70 kms south of Marrakech, this ski resort provides easy and quick access to a variety of high altitude species. Public buses do not run to Oukaïmeden, so a car is essential to reach this site. In winter the road to the resort, especially at higher altitudes, is sometimes temporarily blocked by snow. At this season it will be crowded at week-ends, so a week-day visit recommended.

The approach to the resort is likely to reveal Barbary Partridge, Crag Martin, Dipper and Levaillant's Green Woodpecker. As the road ascends, Black Wheatears and Rock Buntings appear. Once at the resort, Rock Sparrows are very much in evidence, with Black Redstarts of the race *atterrimus* also present. A casual walk should encounter Yellow-billed Choughs, but for a real chough spectacular be there when the early morning sun drops into the valley, when hundreds of choughs swirl down from the surrounding mountain ridges to feed: an unforgettable sight and sound. Lesser numbers of Red-billed

Alpine Accentor

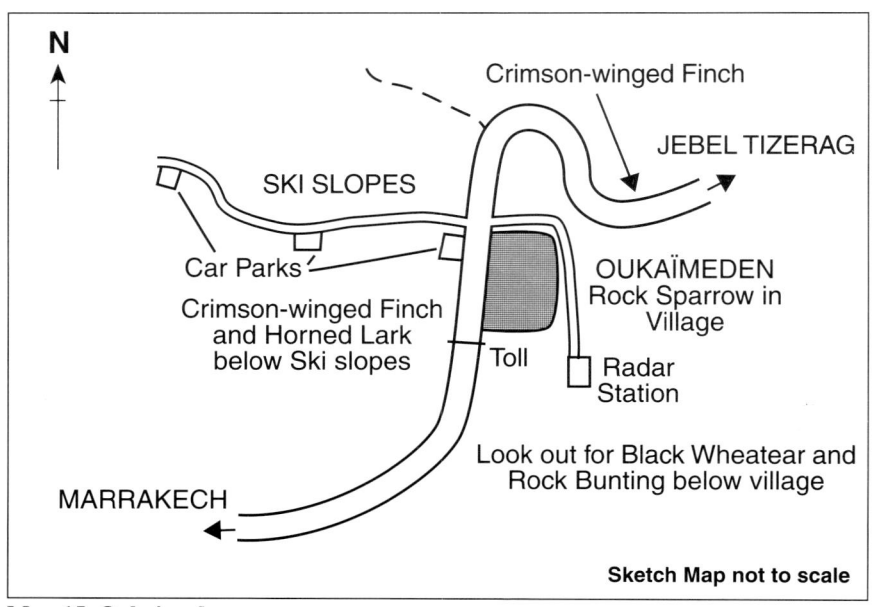

Map 15. Oukaimeden.

Choughs are also present. Dippers can be found by the stream (where else!) and Alpine Accentors winter around the buildings at the upper end of the resort (try the track to the radar station). The road and car parks near the ski lifts are as good as anywhere to look for Horned Lark (of the endemic race *atlas*) and Crimson-winged Finch (of the race *aliena*, also a north African endemic). There is always a possibility of Golden Eagle and Lammergeier here too, although we have to confess that as yet we have failed to encounter either of these dramatic species at this spectacular site.

If you decide to stay overnight, the Chez Ju Ju has a bird logbook and is warm and comfortable with good meals. Being a ski resort, it is inevitably more expensive than some of the hotels you may have stayed in. Be sure to bring warm clothing for this site.

No. 16 The Tizi-n-Test & Tizi-n-Ticka Passes

At some stage of their Moroccan jaunt, most birders use one or other of these passes to cross the High Atlas. Both are spectacular and photogenic, with the Tizi-n-Test providing

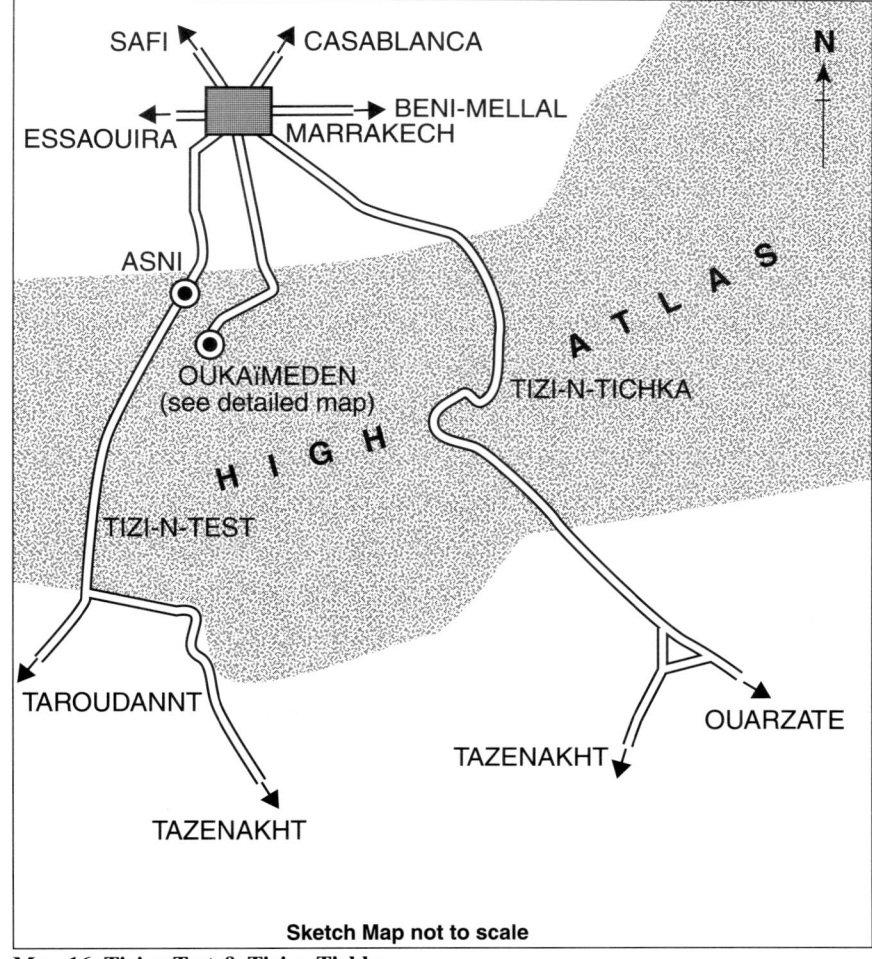

Map 16. Tizi-n-Test & Tizi-n-Tichka.

the more hair-raising journey. Both, too, can be blocked with snow at times. The main Tizi-n-Tichka pass offers the most reliable winter crossing, as snow ploughs regularly operate to keep it open.

Although Oukaïmeden is a better all-round bet for a high altitude species clean-up, good birds can be seen with a bit of luck and persistence. Golden Eagle, Lammergeier, Long-legged Buzzard, Dipper, Horned Lark, Crimson-winged Finch, Tristram's Warbler (summer) and Rock Bunting have all been seen, and the southern approach to the Tizi-n-Tichka seems especially good for Red-billed Chough. Take plenty of film and enjoy the scenery.

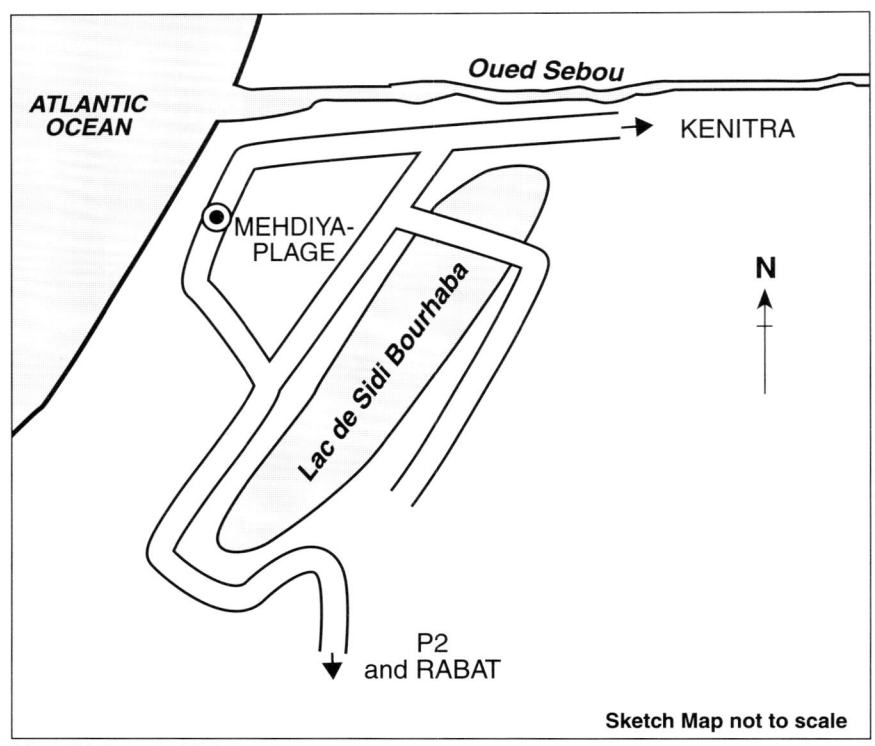

Map 17. Lac de Sidi Bourhaba.

No. 17 LAC DE SIDI BOURHABA

This lagoon, lying behind sand dunes just inland from the Atlantic Ocean, has been a reserve for over twenty years. It is surrounded by woodland which does not always make for easy viewing.

The lagoon can be reached by minor road off the main P2 coast road, either south from the direction of Rabat, or from nearby Kénitra to the north.

Key species here are Marbled Duck (a site of global importance for this threatened duck), Crested Coot and Marsh Owl. Apart from Marbled Duck, this site can also be good for numbers of other wildfowl in winter. Breeding species include Marsh Harrier, Black-winged Stilt and Cetti's Warbler, and during migration periods just about anything can turn up, with a number of North American and sub-Saharan visitors noted. It is also another reasonable spot to get to grips with the north African race of Magpie.

Plate 9. *Cream-coloured Courser*   Hanne & Jens Erikson/Aquila

Plate 10. *Demoiselle Crane*   Conrad Greaves/Aquila

Plate 11. Laughing Dove   Hanne & Jens Erikson/Aquila

Plate 12. Doubled Spurred Francolin   G Dean/Aquila

Plate 13. Hermit Ibis Hans Gebuis/Aquila

Plate 14. Moussiers Redstart Hans Gebuis/Aquila

Plate 15. Crowned Sandgrouse Hanne & Jens Erikson/Aquila

Plate 16. Desert Wheatear Hanne & Jens Erikson/Aquila

Sea-watching hereabouts has produced the usual Northern Gannets, skuas and, on occasion, storm-petrels. The area is an old locality for Slender-billed Curlew.

Just to the north of the lagoon, the Oued Sebou is worth checking-out for waders, gulls and terns.

A Moroccan itinerary visiting some or all of the seventeen areas mentioned in this guide should produce many of the sought-after specialities, and a selection of other species of interest to north European birdwatchers. However, it should be remembered that whilst some species, such as Moussier's Redstart, Thekla Lark and House Bunting are widespread, others are more obscure, and only general areas can be given. The following is an attempt to sketch a background for a handful of those species.

Small Button Quail. An excessively rare resident – claimed extinct in BWP – and unlikely to be recorded by most visitors. May be still possible in the Casablanca – Safi area.

Demoiselle Crane. Although not recorded recently, a small and highly endangered population may survive near Azrou. If you are lucky enough to find these beautiful birds, please treat them with respect and report your sighting to BirdLife International and the Moroccan Ornithological authorities (see address list).

Lichtenstein's Sandgrouse. The fifth sandgrouse species, and confined to the far south of Morocco beyond the Jbel Bani. It's more accessible in Israel!

Plain Swift. Endemic to the Canary and Madeiran archipelagos, this swift has an enigmatic status in north-west Africa. Although lately reliably observed in coastal Morocco in winter, there has also undoubtedly been some confusion with both Common and Pallid Swifts. In short, any swift seen in winter deserves a second glance; the recent paper by Philip Chantler (*Dutch Birding* 15: 97-135) is a useful identification reference. Note too that the species is a potential breeder, with swifts thought to be of this species seen visiting cliff sites between Agadir and Tamri in at least four years between 1988-93.

White-rumped Swift. Recorded mostly from the Atlas south of Marrakech, this late arriving migrant has been seen around Taroudannt, Imlil in the Asni valley, and from the Ourika Valley.

Blue-cheeked Bee-eater. A summer visitor, this species may be sought in the Draa Valley towards Zagora and between Erfoud and Rissani.

Rock Martin. Although the species has bred, its status has been masked by unreliable records. It appears to have been reliably recorded from the Draa Valley in recent times.

Some useful addresses

BirdLife International. Wellbrook Court, Girton Road, Cambridge. CB3 0NA. UK.

British Birds. Mrs Erika Sharrock, BB Subscriptions, Fountains, Park Lane, Blunham, Bedfordshire. MK44 3NJ. UK.

Dutch Birding. Subscription Information: Ron van Enden, c/o Dutch Birding Association, Postbus 75611, 1070 AP Amsterdam, Netherlands.

Morrocan Rare Bird Committee. Dr. Jacques Franchimont, Quartier Abbas, Lmsadhi, rue no 6, no 22, Meknes, Morocco.

Moroccan Tourist Board. 174 Regent Street, London, W1.

Checklist

As explained in the introduction, the names used in this checklist mostly follow the 1993 British Birds list of Western Palearctic birds, with a few later adjustments (e.g. the recognition of Iberian Chiffchaff as a distinct species). It does not purport to be either authoritative or official, and includes species known by us to have been reported but not necessarily yet officially accepted by the Moroccan Rare Birds Committee. Whilst acknowledging that we are open to critisism for this approach, it seems to us that for the purposes of this guide it is both advantageous and forgivable.

We urge all observers who had not yet submitted records of vagrants to the Moroccan Rare Birds Committee to do so, and request that any faults or omissions noted in this checklist are notified to us via the publisher for correction in any future editions. We also look forward to the day when an authoritative avifauna to this marvellous country is produced.

R = Resident **S** = Summer **W** = Winter
M = Migrant **V** = Vagrant **E** = Extinct in Morocco

English name	Scientific name	Status
Red-throated Diver	Gavia stellata	V
Black-throated Diver	Gavia arctica	V
Great Northern Diver	Gavia immer	V
Little Grebe	Tachybaptus ruficollis	R
Great Crested Grebe	Podiceps cristatus	R
Red-necked Grebe	Podiceps grisegena	V
Slavonian Grebe	Podiceps auritus	V
Black-necked Grebe	Podiceps nigricollis	W
Black-browed Albatross	Diomedea melanophris	V
Fulmar	Fulmarus glacialis	V
soft-plumaged petrel	Pterodroma mollis/madeira/feae	V
Bulwer's Petrel	Bulweria bulwerii	V
Cory's Shearwater	Calonectris diomedea	MS
Great Shearwater	Puffinus gravis	M
Sooty Shearwater	Puffinus griseus	M
Manx Shearwater	Puffinus puffinus	MW
Mediterranean Shearwater	Puffinus yelkouan	MW
Little Shearwater	Puffinus assimilis	V
Wilson's Storm-petrel	Oceanites oceanicus	M
White-faced Storm-petrel	Pelagodroma marina	V
European Storm-petrel	Hydrobates pelagicus	MW
Leach's Storm-petrel	Oceanodroma leucorhoa	M
Madeiran Storm-petrel	Oceanodroma castro	V
Red-billed Tropicbird	Phaethon aethereus	V
Masked Booby	Sula dactylatra	V
Brown Booby	Sula leucogaster	V
Northern Gannet	Morus bassana	W
Cape Gannet	Morus capensis	V
Great Cormorant	Phalacrocorax carbo	R
Shag	Phalacrocorax aristotelis	R
Long-tailed Cormorant	Phalacrocorax africanus	V
Darter	Anhinga melanogaster	V
White Pelican	Pelecanus onocrotalus	V

English name	Scientific name	Status
Great Bittern	*Botaurus stellaris*	RMW
Little Bittern	*Ixobrychus minutus*	R
Night Heron	*Nycticorax nycticorax*	S
Squacco Heron	*Ardeola ralloides*	RM
Cattle Egret	*Bubulcus ibis*	R
Western Reef Heron	*Egretta gularis*	V
Little Egret	*Egretta garzetta*	RMW
Great White Egret	*Egretta alba*	V
Grey Heron	*Ardea cinerea*	R
Purple Heron	*Ardea purpurea*	MS
Yellow-billed Stork	*Mycteria ibis*	V
Black Stork	*Ciconia nigra*	M
White Stork	*Ciconia ciconia*	MS
Glossy Ibis	*Plegadis falcinellus*	W
Bald Ibis	*Geronticus eremita*	R
Eurasian Spoonbill	*Platalea leucorodia*	W
Greater Flamingo	*Phoenicopterus ruber*	MSW
Lesser Flamingo	*Phoenicopterus minor*	V
Fulvous Whistling Duck	*Dendrocygna bicolor*	V
Mute Swan	*Cygnus olor*	V
Tundra Swan	*Cygnus columbianus*	V
Whooper Swan	*Cygnus cygnus*	W
Bean Goose	*Anser fabalis*	V
White-fronted Goose	*Anser albifrons*	V
Greylag Goose	*Anser anser*	W
Snow Goose	*Anser caerulescens*	V
Barnacle Goose	*Branta leucopsis*	V
Brent Goose	*Branta bernicla*	V
Ruddy Shelduck	*Tadorna ferruginea*	R
Common Shelduck	*Tadorna tadorna*	W
Spur-winged Goose	*Plectropterus gambensis*	V
Mandarin Duck	*Aix galericulata*	V
Eurasian Wigeon	*Anas penelope*	W
American Wigeon	*Anas americana*	V
Gadwall	*Anas strepera*	W
Common Teal	*Anas crecca*	W
Mallard	*Anas platyrhynchos*	R
Northern Pintail	*Anas acuta*	R
Garganey	*Anas querquedula*	M
Blue-winged Teal	*Anas discors*	V
Northern Shoveler	*Anas clypeata*	W
Cape Shoveler	*Anas smithii*	V
Marbled Duck	*Marmaronetta angustirostris*	R
Red-crested Pochard	*Netta rufina*	W
Common Pochard	*Aythya ferina*	W
Ring-necked Duck	*Aythya collaris*	V
Ferruginous Duck	*Aythya nyroca*	M
Tufted Duck	*Aythya fuligula*	W
Greater Scaup	*Aythya marila*	V
Common Scoter	*Melanitta nigra*	W
Velvet Scoter	*Melanitta fusca*	V

English name	Scientific name	Status
Common Goldeneye	*Bucephala clangula*	V
Red-breasted Merganser	*Mergus serrator*	W
Goosander	*Mergus merganser*	V
Ruddy Duck	*Oxyura jamaicensis*	V
White-headed Duck	*Oxyura leucocephala*	W
Honey-buzzard	*Pernis apivorus*	M
Black-shouldered Kite	*Elanus caeruleus*	R
Black Kite	*Milvus migrans*	S
Red Kite	*Milvus milvus*	R
Lammergeier	*Gypaetus barbatus*	R
Egyptian Vulture	*Neophron percnopterus*	RM
Hooded Vulture	*Necrosyrtes monachus*	V
Griffon Vulture	*Gyps fulvus*	MW
Lappet-faced Vulture	*Torgos tracheliotus*	V
Monk Vulture	*Aegypius monachus*	V
Short-toed Eagle	*Circaetus gallicus*	MS
Marsh Harrier	*Circus aeruginosus*	RMW
Hen Harrier	*Circus cyaneus*	W
Pallid Harrier	*Circus macrourus*	V
Montagu's Harrier	*Circus pygargus*	MS
Dark Chanting Goshawk	*Melierax metabates*	R
Northern Goshawk	*Accipiter gentilis*	RW
Eurasian Sparrowhawk	*Accipiter nisus*	RW
Common Buzzard	*Buteo buteo*	MW
Long-legged Buzzard	*Buteo rufinus*	R
Spotted Eagle	*Aquila clanga*	V
Tawny Eagle	*Aquila rapax*	R
Imperial Eagle	*Aquila heliaca*	V
Golden Eagle	*Aquila chrysaetos*	R
Booted Eagle	*Hieraaetus pennatus*	MS
Bonelli's Eagle	*Hieraaetus fasciatus*	R
Osprey	*Pandion haliaetus*	RMW
Lesser Kestrel	*Falco naumanni*	MS
Common Kestrel	*Falco tinnunculus*	RW
Red-footed Falcon	*Falco vespertinus*	V
Merlin	*Falco columbarius*	W
Hobby	*Falco subbuteo*	MS
Eleonora's Falcon	*Falco eleonorae*	S
Lanner Falcon	*Falco biarmicus*	R
Saker Falcon	*Falco cherrug*	V
Peregrine Falcon	*Falco peregrinus*	RW
Barbary Falcon	*Falco pelegrinoides*	R
Barbary Partridge	*Alectoris barbara*	R
Double-spurred Francolin	*Francolinus bicalcaratus*	R
Quail	*Coturnix coturnix*	MS
Common Pheasant	*Phasianus colchicus*	R
Helmeted Guineafowl	*Numida meleagris*	E
Small Button-quail	*Turnix sylvatica*	E?
Water Rail	*Rallus aquaticus*	RW
Spotted Crake	*Porzana porzana*	M
Little Crake	*Porzana parva*	M

English name	Scientific name	Status
Baillon's Crake	*Porzana pusilla*	MS
Corn Crake	*Crex crex*	W
Moorhen	*Gallinula chloropus*	R
Allen's Gallinule	*Porphyrula alleni*	V
Purple Swamp-hen	*Porphyrio porphyrio*	R
Common Coot	*Fulica atra*	RW
Crested Coot	*Fulica cristata*	R
Common Crane	*Grus grus*	W
Demoiselle Crane	*Anthropoides virgo*	E?
Little Bustard	*Tetrax tetrax*	RW
Houbara Bustard	*Chlamydotis undulata*	R
Arabian Bustard	*Ardeotis arabs*	E?
Great Bustard	*Otis tarda*	R
Oystercatcher	*Haematopus ostralegus*	MW
Black-winged Stilt	*Himantopus himantopus*	RMW
Avocet	*Recurvirostra avosetta*	MSW
Stone-curlew	*Burhinus oedicnemus*	RW
Egyptian Courser	*Pluvianus aegyptius*	V
Cream-coloured Courser	*Cursorius cursor*	R
Collared Pratincole	*Glareola pratincola*	MSW
Black-winged Pratincole	*Glareola nordmanni*	V
Little Ringed Plover	*Charadrius dubius*	RM
Great Ringed Plover	*Charadrius hiaticula*	MW
Kittlitz's Plover	*Charadrius pecuarius*	V
Kentish Plover	*Charadrius alexandrinus*	RW
Greater Sand Plover	*Charadrius leschenaultii*	V
Dotterel	*Charadrius morinellus*	W
American Golden Plover	*Pluvialis dominica*	V
Golden Plover	*Pluvialis apricaria*	W
Grey Plover	*Pluvialis squatarola*	MW
Sociable Lapwing	*Chettusia gregaria*	V
White-tailed Lapwing	*Chettusia leucura*	V
Northern Lapwing	*Vanellus vanellus*	RW
Great Knot	*Calidris tenuirostris*	V
Red Knot	*Calidris canutus*	W
Semipalmated Sandpiper	*Calidris pusilla*	V
Sanderling	*Calidris alba*	MW
Little Stint	*Calidris minuta*	MW
Temminck's Stint	*Calidris temminckii*	MW
Pectoral Sandpiper	*Calidris melanotos*	V
Curlew Sandpiper	*Calidris ferruginea*	M
Purple Sandpiper	*Calidris maritima*	V
Dunlin	*Calidris alpina*	MW
Broad-billed Sandpiper	*Limicola falcinellus*	V
Stilt Sandpiper	*Micropalma himantopus*	V
Ruff	*Philomachus pugnax*	MW
Jack Snipe	*Lymnocryptes minimus*	MW
Common Snipe	*Gallinago gallinago*	MW
Great Snipe	*Gallinago media*	MW
Long-billed Dowitcher	*Limnodromus griseus*	V
Woodcock	*Scolopax rusticola*	W

				English name	Scientific name	Status
				Black-tailed Godwit	*Limosa limosa*	MW
				Bar-tailed Godwit	*Limosa lapponica*	MW
				Whimbrel	*Numenius phaeopus*	MW
				Slender-billed Curlew	*Numenius tenuirostris*	W
				Eurasian Curlew	*Numenius arquata*	MW
				Spotted Redshank	*Tringa erythropus*	MW
				Common Redshank	*Tringa totanus*	MW
				Marsh Sandpiper	*Tringa stagnatilis*	M
				Common Greenshank	*Tringa nebularia*	MW
				Lesser Yellowlegs	*Tringa flaviceps*	V
				Green Sandpiper	*Tringa ochropus*	MW
				Wood Sandpiper	*Tringa glareola*	MW
				Common Sandpiper	*Actitis hypoleucos*	MW
				Spotted Sandpiper	*Actitis macularia*	V
				Turnstone	*Arenaria interpres*	MW
				Wilson's Phalarope	*Phalaropus tricolor*	V
				Red-necked Phalarope	*Phalaropus lobatus*	W
				Grey Phalarope	*Phalaropus fulicarius*	W
				Pomarine Skua	*Stercorarius pomarinus*	MW
				Arctic Skua	*Stercorarius parasiticus*	MW
				Long-tailed Skua	*Stercorarius longicaudus*	V
				Great Skua	*Stercorarius skua*	MW
				Mediterranean Gull	*Larus melanocephalus*	W
				Laughing Gull	*Larus atricilla*	V
				Franklin's Gull	*Larus pipixcan*	V
				Little Gull	*Larus minutus*	MW
				Sabine's Gull	*Larus sabini*	M
				Black-headed Gull	*Larus ridibundus*	W
				Grey-headed Gull	*Larus cirrocephalus*	V
				Slender-billed Gull	*Larus genei*	R
				Audouin's Gull	*Larus audouinii*	RW
				Ring-billed Gull	*Larus delawarensis*	V
				Common Gull	*Larus canus*	W
				Lesser Black-backed Gull	*Larus fuscus*	MW
				Herring Gull	*Larus argentatus*	W
				Yellow-legged Gull	*Larus cachinnans*	R
				Iceland Gull	*Larus glaucoides*	V
				Glaucous Gull	*Larus hyperboreus*	V
				Great Black-backed Gull	*Larus marinus*	W
				Glaucous-winged Gull	*Larus glaucescens*	V
				Kittiwake	*Rissa tridactyla*	W
				Gull-billed Tern	*Gelochelidon nilotica*	MS
				Caspian Tern	*Sterna caspia*	MW
				Royal Tern	*Sterna maxima*	MW
				Lesser Crested Tern	*Sterna bengalensis*	MW
				Sandwich Tern	*Sterna sandvicensis*	MW
				Roseate Tern	*Sterna dougallii*	M
				Common Tern	*Sterna hirundo*	MSW
				Arctic Tern	*Sterna paradisaea*	M
				Little Tern	*Sterna albifrons*	MS
				Whiskered Tern	*Chlidonias hybridus*	MW

English name	Scientific name	Status
Black Tern	*Chlidonias niger*	M
White-winged Black Tern	*Chlidonias leucopterus*	M
Common Guillemot	*Uria aalge*	V
Razorbill	*Alca torda*	W
Puffin	*Fratercula arctica*	W
Lichtenstein's Sandgrouse	*Pterocles lichtensteinii*	R
Crowned Sandgrouse	*Pterocles coronatus*	R
Spotted Sandgrouse	*Pterocles senegallus*	R
Black-bellied Sandgrouse	*Pterocles orientalis*	R
Pin-tailed Sandgrouse	*Pterocles alchata*	R
Rock Dove	*Columba livia*	R
Stock Dove	*Columba oenas*	R
Wood Pigeon	*Columba palumbus*	RW
Collared Dove	*Streptopelia decaocto*	R
Turtle Dove	*Streptopelia turtur*	MS
Laughing Dove	*Streptopelia senegalensis*	R
Namaqua Dove	*Oena capensis*	V
Great Spotted Cuckoo	*Clamator glandarius*	M
Common Cuckoo	*Cuculus canorus*	MS
Yellow-billed Cuckoo	*Coccyzus americanus*	V
Barn Owl	*Tyto alba*	R
Eurasian Scops Owl	*Otus scops*	MS
Eagle Owl	*Bubo bubo*	R
Little Owl	*Athene noctua*	R
Tawny Owl	*Strix aluco*	R
Long-eared Owl	*Asio otus*	MW
Short-eared Owl	*Asio flammeus*	MW
Marsh Owl	*Asio capensis*	R
European Nightjar	*Caprimulgus europaeus*	MS
Red-necked Nightjar	*Caprimulgus ruficollis*	MS
Egyptian Nightjar	*Caprimulgus aegyptius*	S
Plain Swift	*Apus unicolor*	W?
Common Swift	*Apus apus*	MSW
Pallid Swift	*Apus pallidus*	MSW
Alpine Swift	*Apus melba*	MS
White-rumped Swift	*Apus caffer*	S
Little Swift	*Apus affinis*	MSW
Common Kingfisher	*Alcedo atthis*	RW
Blue-cheeked Bee-eater	*Merops superciliosus*	S
European Bee-eater	*Merops apiaster*	MS
European Roller	*Coracias garrulus*	MS
Hoopoe	*Upupa epops*	MS
Wryneck	*Jynx torquilla*	MW
Levaillant's Green Woodpecker	*Picus vaillantii*	R
Great Spotted Woodpecker	*Dendrocopos major*	R
Black-crowned Sparrow Lark	*Eremopterix nigriceps*	V
Bar-tailed Desert Lark	*Ammomanes cincturus*	R
Desert Lark	*Ammomanes deserti*	R
Hoopoe Lark	*Alaemon alaudipes*	R
Dupont's Lark	*Chersophilus duponti*	R
Thick-billed Lark	*Rhamphocoris clotbey*	R

English name	Scientific name	Status
Calandra Lark	*Melanocorypha calandra*	R
Short-toed Lark	*Calandrella brachydactyla*	S
Lesser Short-toed Lark	*Calandrella rufescens*	R
Crested Lark	*Galerida cristata*	R
Thekla Lark	*Galerida theklae*	R
Wood Lark	*Lullula arborea*	R
Sky Lark	*Alauda arvensis*	RW
Horned Lark	*Eremophila alpestris*	R
Temminck's Horned Lark	*Eremophila bilopha*	R
Plain Martin	*Riparia paludicola*	R
Sand Martin	*Riparia riparia*	MS
Rock Martin	*Ptyonoprogne fuligula*	R
Crag Martin	*Ptyonoprogne rupestris*	RW
Barn Swallow	*Hirundo rustica*	MS
Red-rumped Swallow	*Hirundo daurica*	MS
House Martin	*Delichon urbica*	MS
Richard's Pipit	*Anthus novaeseelandiae*	V
Tawny Pipit	*Anthus campestris*	MS
Tree Pipit	*Anthus trivialis*	M
Meadow Pipit	*Anthus pratensis*	W
Red-throated Pipit	*Anthus cervinus*	MW
Water Pipit	*Anthus spinoletta*	W
Rock Pipit	*Anthus petrosus*	W
Yellow Wagtail	*Motacilla flava*	MSW
Grey Wagtail	*Motacilla cinerea*	RW
Pied Wagtail	*Motacilla alba*	RW
Garden Bulbul	*Pycnonotus barbatus*	R
Dipper	*Cinclus cinclus*	R
Wren	*Troglodytes troglodytes*	R
Hedge Accentor	*Prunella modularis*	V
Alpine Accentor	*Prunella collaris*	RW
Rufous-tailed Scrub-robin	*Cercotrichas galactotes*	S
Robin	*Erithacus rubecula*	RW
Rufous Nightingale	*Luscinia megarhynchos*	MS
Bluethroat	*Luscinia svecica*	MW
Black Redstart	*Phoenicurus ochruros*	RW
Common Redstart	*Phoenicurus phoenicurus*	MS
Moussier's Redstart	*Phoenicurus moussieri*	R
Whinchat	*Saxicola rubetra*	M
Common Stonechat	*Saxicola torquata*	RW
Isabelline Wheatear	*Oenanthe isabellina*	V
Northern Wheatear	*Oenanthe oenanthe*	RMS
Black-eared Wheatear	*Oenanthe hispanica*	MS
Desert Wheatear	*Oenanthe deserti*	RS
Red-rumped Wheatear	*Oenanthe moesta*	R
Mourning Wheatear	*Oenanthe lugens*	R
White-crowned Black Wheatear	*Oenanthe leucopyga*	R
Black Wheatear	*Oenanthe leucura*	R
Rock Thrush	*Monticola saxatilis*	MS
Blue Rock Thrush	*Monticola solitarius*	R
Ring Ouzel	*Turdus torquatus*	W

English name	Scientific name	Status
Blackbird	*Turdus merula*	R
Fieldfare	*Turdus pilaris*	V
Song Thrush	*Turdus philomelos*	MW
Redwing	*Turdus iliacus*	W
Mistle Thrush	*Turdus viscivorus*	RW
Cetti's Warbler	*Cettia cetti*	R
Zitting Cisticola	*Cisticola juncidis*	R
Streaked Scrub Warbler	*Scotocerca inquieta*	R
Grasshopper Warbler	*Locustella naevia*	MW
River Warbler	*Locustella fluviatilis*	V
Savi's Warbler	*Locustella luscinioides*	MS
Moustached Warbler	*Acrocephalus melanopogon*	R
Aquatic Warbler	*Acrocephalus paludicola*	M
Sedge Warbler	*Acrocephalus schoenobaenus*	M
Marsh Warbler	*Acrocephalus palustris*	V
Reed Warbler	*Acrocephalus scirpaceus*	MS
Great Reed Warbler	*Acrocephalus arundinaceus*	MS
Olivaceous Warbler	*Hippolais pallida*	MS
Icterine Warbler	*Hippolais icterina*	V
Melodious Warbler	*Hippolais polyglotta*	MS
Marmora's Warbler	*Sylvia sarda*	V
Dartford Warbler	*Sylvia undata*	R
Tristram's Warbler	*Sylvia deserticola*	R
Spectacled Warbler	*Sylvia conspicillata*	R
Subalpine Warbler	*Sylvia cantillans*	MS
Sardinian Warbler	*Sylvia melanocephala*	R
Desert Warbler	*Sylvia nana*	R
Orphean Warbler	*Sylvia hortensis*	MS
Lesser Whitethroat	*Sylvia curruca*	V
Whitethroat	*Sylvia communis*	MS
Garden Warbler	*Sylvia borin*	M
Blackcap	*Sylvia atricapilla*	RMW
Radde's Warbler	*Phylloscopus schwarzi*	V
Dusky Warbler	*Phylloscopus fuscatus*	V
Western Bonelli's Warbler	*Phylloscopus bonelli*	MS
Wood Warbler	*Phylloscopus sibilatrix*	M
Chiffchaff	*Phylloscopus collybita*	RMW
Iberian Chiffchaff	*Phylloscopus brehmii*	RW
Willow Warbler	*Phylloscopus trochilus*	M
Goldcrest	*Regulus regulus*	V
Firecrest	*Regulus ignicapillus*	R
Spotted Flycatcher	*Muscicapa striata*	MS
Pied Flycatcher	*Ficedula hypoleuca*	MS
Semi-collared Flycatcher	*Ficedula semitorquata*	V
Collared Flycatcher	*Ficedula albicollis*	V
Red-breasted Flycatcher	*Ficedula parva*	V
Bearded Tit	*Panurus biarmicus*	V
Fulvous Babbler	*Turdoides fulvus*	R
Long-tailed Tit	*Aegithalos caudatus*	V
Crested Tit	*Parus cristatus*	V
Coal Tit	*Parus ater*	R

English name	Scientific name	Status
Blue Tit	*Parus caeruleus*	R
Great Tit	*Parus major*	R
Wood Nuthatch	*Sitta europaea*	R
Wallcreeper	*Tichodroma muraria*	V
Short-toed Treecreeper	*Certhia brachydactyla*	R
Penduline Tit	*Remiz pendulinus*	V
Golden Oriole	*Oriolus oriolus*	MS
Black-crowned Tchagra	*Tchagra senegala*	R
Red-backed Shrike	*Lanius collurio*	V
Southern Grey Shrike	*Lanius meridionalis*	R
Woodchat Shrike	*Lanius senator*	MS
Eurasian Jay	*Garrulus glandarius*	R
Magpie	*Pica pica*	R
Yellow-billed Chough	*Pyrrhocorax graculus*	R
Red-billed Chough	*Pyrrhocorax pyrrhocorax*	R
Eurasian Jackdaw	*Corvus monedula*	R
Carrion Crow	*Corvus corone*	V
Brown-necked Raven	*Corvus ruficollis*	R
Common Raven	*Corvus corax*	R
Common Starling	*Sturnus vulgaris*	W
Spotless Starling	*Sturnus unicolor*	R
House Sparrow	*Passer domesticus*	R
Spanish Sparrow	*Passer hispaniolensis*	R
Desert Sparrow	*Passer simplex*	R
Tree Sparrow	*Passer montanus*	V
Rock Sparrow	*Petronia petronia*	R
Senegal Firefinch	*Lagonosticta senegala*	V
Red-eyed Vireo	*Vireo olivaceus*	V
Chaffinch	*Fringilla coelebs*	RW
Brambling	*Fringilla montifringilla*	W
European Serin	*Serinus serinus*	RW
Greenfinch	*Carduelis chloris*	RW
Goldfinch	*Carduelis carduelis*	RW
Siskin	*Carduelis spinus*	W
Linnet	*Acanthis cannabina*	RW
Common Redpoll	*Acanthis flammea*	V
Common Crossbill	*Loxia curvirostra*	RW
Crimson-winged Finch	*Rhodopechys sanguinea*	R
Trumpeter Finch	*Bucanetes githagineus*	R
Common Rosefinch	*Carpodacus erythrinus*	V
Bullfinch	*Pyrrhula pyrrhula*	V
Hawfinch	*Coccothraustes coccothraustes*	RW
Snow Bunting	*Plectophenax nivalis*	V
Pine Bunting	*Emberiza leucocephalus*	V
Cirl Bunting	*Emberiza cirlus*	R
Rock Bunting	*Emberiza cia*	R
House Bunting	*Emberiza striolata*	R
Ortolan Bunting	*Emberiza hortulana*	M
Little Bunting	*Emberiza pusilla*	V
Reed Bunting	*Emberiza schoeniclus*	RW
Black-headed Bunting	*Emberiza melanocephala*	V

ADDITIONAL SPECIES

				Corn Bunting	*Miliaria calandra*	R

OTHER WILDLIFE

Apart from birds, Morocco has much to offer the keen European naturalist, thus we have prepared checklists covering three of the more accessible groups: mammals, butterflies and dragonflies.

As with the bird checklist, we would be interested to have comment on any errors or omissions noted by users of this guide, so we can correct them in any future edition. Any comments should be sent to the authors via the publisher.

MAMMALS

Several interesting sub-species of mammal are found in north Africa. The Red Fox for example is represented by two forms: the Barbary Red in coastal Morocco, and the Atlantic Red in the region of the Atlas. Other examples are provided by the Numidian Weasel, which occurs north of the Atlas Mountains, and the African Polecat, a sub-species of the European or Western Polecat.

As elsewhere, many types of mammal are very scarce or even rare nowadays, and some, including Leopard, Serval and Mediterranean Monk Seal, are almost certainly extinct. On the other hand, others such as the introduced Spanish Red Deer survive well and prosper. These Red Deer can be found between Ceuta and Tanger, where they were introduced in 1952.

While some of the mammals listed are relatively easy to see (e.g. Wild Boar at Oued Massa), you will require more than a little luck with others such as the cetaceans and the bats. Names follow those used in *A Field Guide to the Mammals of Africa* (Haltenorth & Diller) Collins, London, 1980 and *Mammals of Britain and Europe* (Macdonald & Barrett) Collins, London, 1993.

English name	Scientific name
Wild Boar	*Sus scrofa*
Spanish Red Deer	*Cervus elaphus hispanicus*
Dorcas Gazelle	*Gazella dorcas*
Edmi Gazelle	*Gazella gazella cuvieri*
Barbary Sheep	*Ammotragus lervia*
Barbary Ground Squirrel	*Atlantoxerus gentulus*
Geoffroy's Ground Squirrel	*Euxerus erythropus*
North African Crested Porcupine	*Hystrix cristata*
Gundi	*Ctenodactylus gundi*
Wood Mouse	*Apodemus sylvaticus*
Black Rat	*Rattus rattus*
Algerian Mouse	*Mus spretus*
House Mouse	*Mus musculus domesticus*
European Rabbit	*Oryetolagus cuniculus*
Cape or Brown Hare	*Lepus capensis*
Mediterranean Monk Seal	*Monachus monachus*
Barbary Red Fox	*Vulpes vulpes barbarus*
Atlantic Red Fox	*Vulpes vulpes atlanticus*
Golden Jackal	*Canis aureus Numidian*
Weasel	*Mustela nivalis numidica*
African Polecat	*Mustela putoris furo*
Libyan Striped Weasel	*Poecilictis libyva*
Ratel or Honey Badger	*Mellivora Capensis*
North African Otter	*Lutra lutra angustifrons*
Small Spotted or Common Genet	*Genetta genetta*
Egyptian Mongoose	*Herpestes ichneumon*

					English name	Scientific name
					Berber Striped Hyena	*Hyaena hyaena barbara*
					Leopard	*Panthera pardus*
					Caracal	*Caracal caracal*
					Serval	*Leptailurus serval*
					Sand Cat	*Felis margarita*
					African Wildcat or Kaffir Cat	*Felis silvestris*
					Barbary Ape	*Macaca sylvana*
					Algerian Hedgehog	*Erinaceus algirus*
					Desert Hedgehog	*Paraechinus aethiopicus*
					Greater White-toothed Shrew	*Crocidura russula*
					North African Elephant Shrew	*Elephantulus rozeti*
					Lesser Horseshoe Bat	*Rhinolophus hipposideros*
					Greater Horseshoe Bat	*Rhinolophus ferrumequinum*
					Natterer's Bat	*Myotis nattereri*
					Common Pipistrelle	*Pipistrellus pipistrellus*
					Noctule	*Nyctalus noctula*
					Serotine Bat	*Eptesicus serotinus*
					Grey Long-eared Bat	*Plecotus austriacus*
					Rough-toothed Dolphin	*Steno bredanensis*
					Striped Dolphin	*Stenella coeruleoalba*
					Atlantic Spotted Dolphin	*Stenella frontalis*
					Common Dolphin	*Delphinus delphis*
					Bottle-nosed Dolhin	*Tursiops truncatus*
					False Killer Whale	*Pseudorca crassidens*
					Killer Whale	*Orcinus orca*
					Risso's Dolphin	*Grampus griseus*
					Long-finned Pilor Whale	*Globicephala melaena*
					Harbour Porpoise	*Phocoena phocoena*
					Dwarf Sperm Whale	*Kogia simus*
					Sowerby's Beaked Whale	*Mesoplodon bidens*
					Cuvier's Beaked Whale	*Ziphius cavirostris*
					Blue Whale	*Balaenoptera musculus*
					Fin Whale	*Balaenoptera physalus Sei*
					Whale	*Balaenoptera borealis*
					Minke Whale	*Balaenoptera acutorostrata*
					Humpback Whale	*Megaptera novaeangliae*
					Northern Right Whale	*Eubalaena glacialis*

DRAGONFLIES

The Odonata-damselflies and dragonflies – are well represented in Morocco, and these eye-catching and graceful insects offer wide scope for study and discovery. Remember that this group of insects are great migrants, so other species from sub-Saharan Africa not mentioned in this list are always possible.

As with other groups of flora and fauna there are a number of North African sub-species to be found, including Southern and Azure Damselflies, and Golden-ringed Dragonfly. *Cordulegaster princeps* (a species similar to Golden-ringed Dragonfly) is endemic to the Atlas Mountains.

Both the English and scientific names used in this checklist conform to those in the only practical guide covering north African dragonflies: *A Field Guide to the Dragonflies of Britain, Europe and North Africa* (d'Aguilar, Dommanget & Prechac), Collins, London, 1986. Thus it should be born in mind that these names may differ in some cases from those adopted by more recent, specialist, and less widely available dragonfly literature. As many of these insects do not have vernacular English names, scientific names are given first with English names, if applicable, added in brackets.

Scientific name	English name
Calopteryx haemorrhoidalis	(Mediterranean Demoiselle)
Calopteryx virgo meridionalis	(Beautiful Demoiselle)
Calopteryx exul	
Sympecma fusca	(Common Winter Damselfly)
Lestes barbarus	(Southern Emerald Damselfly)
Lestes virens	(Small Emerald Damselfly)
Lestes viridis	(Willow Emerald Damselfly)
Lestes sponsa	(Emerald Damselfly)
Lestes dryas	(Scarce Emerald Damselfly)
Platycnem is subdila ta ta	
Pyrrhosoma nymphula	(Large Red Damselfly)
Ischnura saharensis	
Ischnura pumilio	(Scarce Blue-tailed Damselfly)
Ischnura graellsii	
Ischnura fountainei	
Coenagrion lindenii	(Goblet-marked Damselfly)
Coenagrion scitulum	(Dainty Damselfly)
Coenagrion mercuriale hermeticum	(Southern Damselfly)
Coenagrion caerulescens	
Coenagrion puella kocheri	(Azure Damselfly)
Enallagma deserti	
Erythromma viridulum	(Small Red-eyed Damselfly)
Ceriagrion tenellum nielseni	(Small Red Damselfly)
Gomphus simillimus	(Yellow Club-tailed Dragonfly)
Gomphus lucasii	
Paragomphus genei	
Onychogomphus forcipatus	(Green-eyed Hook-tailed Dragonfly)
Onychogomphus uncatus	(Blue-eyed Hook-tailed Dragonfly)
Onychogomphus costae	
Boyeria irene	(Crepuscular Hawker)
Aeshna cyanea	(Southern Hawker)
Aeshna mixta	(Migrant Hawker)
Aeshna affinis	(Mediterranean Hawker)
Anaciaeschna isosceles	(Norfolk Hawker)

					Scientific name	English name
					Hemianax ephippiger	(Vagrant Emperor Dragonfly)
					Anax imperator	(Emperor Dragonfly)
					Anax parthenope	(Lesser Emperor Dragonfly)
					Cordulegaster boltonii algericas	(Golden-ringed Dragonfly)
					Cordulegaster princeps	
					Libellula quadrimaculata	(Four-spotted Chaser)
					Orthetrum cancellatum	(Black-tailed Skimmer)
					Orthetrum brunneum	(Southern Skimmer)
					Orthetrum trinacria	
					Orthetrum chrysostigma	
					Orthetrum nitidinerve	
					Orthetrum anceps	
					Diplacodes lefebvrii	
					Crocothemis erythraea	(Scarlet Darter)
					Brachythemis leucosticta	
					Sympetrum sanguineum	(Ruddy Darter)
					Sympetrum fonscolombii	(Red-veined Darter)
					Sympetrum meridionale	(Southern Darter)
					Sympetrum striolatum	(Common Darter)
					Zygonyx torrida	
					Trithemis annulata	
					Trithemis arteriosa	
					Trithemis kirbyi ardens	
					Selysiothemis nigra	

BUTTERFLIES

Not suprisingly, Morocco is rich in butterflies, with two species endemic to the country: Vogel's Blue is found only in the Middle Atlas at its type locality around the Taghzeft Pass, while the Atlas Blue also occurs there as well as at Jebel Toubkal in the High Atlas.

British butterfly enthusiasts will soon discover that Morocco holds an array of familiar species, but that these are represented by unfamiliar forms: there are two sub-species of Meadow Brown and Glanville Fritillary to be seen, and Dark Green Fritillary, Green-veined White and Lulworth and Essex Skippers are other examples. As with both dragonflies and birds, vagrants from further south in Africa can and do turn up.

We can wholeheartedly recommend the expert text, illustrations and maps of A *Field Guide to the Butterflies of Britain and Europe* (Higgins, Riley & Hargreaves), 5th Edition, Collins, London, 1993. We have therefore followed both the vernacular and scientific names used in that guide in this checklist.

			Scientific name	English name
			Swallowtail	*Papilio machaon*
			Scarce Swallowtail	*Iphiclides podalirius feisthamelii*
			Spanish Festoon	*Zerynthia rumina ornatior*
			Black-veined White	*Aporia crataegi*
			Large White	*Pieris brassicae*
			Small White	*Artogeia rapae*
			Southern Small White	*Artogeia mannii*
			Green-veined White	*Artogeia napi atlantis*
			Bath White	*Pontia daplidice*
			Dappled White	*Euchloe simplonia*
			Portuguese Dappled White	*Euchloe tagis tagis*
			Scarce Green-striped White	*Euchloe falloui*
			Green-striped White	*Euchloe belemia belemia*
			Greenish Black-tip	*Elphinstonia charlonia charlonia*
			Morocco Orange Tip	*Anthocharis belia belia*
			Sooty Orange Tip	*Zegris eupheme meridionalis*
			Desert Orange Tip	*Colotis evagore*
			Clouded Yellow	*Colias crocea*
			Brimstone	*Gonepteryx rhamni*
			Cleopatra	*Gonepteryx cleopatra cleopatra*
			Wood White	*Leptidea sinapis*
			Donzel's Silver-line	*Cigaritis zohra*
			Allard's Silver-line	*Cigaritis allardi*
			Purple Hairstreak	*Quercusia quercus ibericus*
			False Ilex Hairstreak	*Nordmannia esculi mauretanica*
			Green Hairstreak	*Callophrys rubi*
			Chapman's Green Hairstreak	*Callophrys avis*
			Provence Hairstreak	*Tomares ballus*
			Moroccan Hairstreak	*Tomares mauretanicus*
			Small Copper	*Lyvaena Phlaeas*
			Purple-shot Copper	*Heodes alciphron heracleanus*
			Moroccan Copper	*Thersamonia phoebus*
			Long-tailed Blue	*Lampides boeticus*
			Lang's Short-tailed Blue	*Syntarucus pirithous*
			Common Tiger Blue	*Tarucus theophrastus*
			Mediterranean Tiger Blue	*Tarucus rosaceus*
			African Babul Blue	*Azanus jesous*

English name	Scientific name
African Grass Blue	*Zizeeria knysna knysna*
Lorquin's Blue	*Cupido lorquinii*
Holly Blue	*Celastrina argiolus*
Black-eyed Blue	*Glaucopsyche melanops algirica*
Iolas Blue	*Iolana iolas*
False Baton Blue	*Pseuclophilotes abencerragus*
Bavius Blue	*Pseudophilotes bavius*
Vogel's Blue	*Plebejus vogelii*
Martin's Blue	*Plebejus martini martini*
Brown Argus	*Aricia agestis cramera*
Mountain Argus	*Aricia artaxerxes montensis*
Mazarine Blue	*Cyaniris semiargus*
Escher's Blue	*Agrodiaetus escheri ahmar*
Amanda's Blue	*Agrodiaetus amanda abdelazk*
Chapman's Blue	*Agrodiaetus thersites*
Atlas Blue	*Plebicula atlantica*
Spanish Chalk-hill Blue	*Lysandra albicans berber*
Spotted Adonis Blue	*Lysandra punctifera*
Common Blue	*Polyommatus icarus*
Two-tailed Pasha	*Charaxes jasius*
Large Tortoiseshell	*Nymphalis polychloros erythromelas*
Red Admiral	*Vanessa atalanta*
Painted Lady	*Cynthia cardui*
Comma	*Polygonia c-album*
Cardinal	*Pandoriana pandora*
Dark Green Fritillary	*Mesoacidalia aglaja Iyauteyi*
Niobe Fritillary	*Fabriciana niobe auresiana*
Queen of Spain Fritillary	*Issoria lathonia*
Glanville Fritillary	*Melitaea cinxia cinxia*
Glanville Fritillary	*Melitaea cinxia atlantis*
Knapweed Fritillary	*Melitaea phoebe punica*
Aetherie Fritillary	*Melitaea aetherie algirica*
Spotted Fritillary	*Melitaea didyma occidentalis*
Desert Fritillary	*Melitaea deserticola*
Provencal Fritillary	*Mellicta deione nitida*
Marsh Fritillary	*Eurodryas aurinia beckeri*
Spanish Fritillary	*Eurodryas desfontainii desfontainii*
Marbled White	*Melanargia galathea lucasi*
Western Marbled White	*Melanargia occitanica pelagia*
Spanish Marbled White	*Melanargia ines*
Rock Grayling	*Hipparchia alcyone caroli*
Southern Grayling	*Hipparchia aristaeus algiricus*
Tree Grayling	*Neohipparchia statilinus sylvicola*
Austaut's Grayling	*Neohipparchia hansii*
Striped Grayling	*Pseudotergumiafidia*
The Hermit	*Chazara briseis*
Southern Hermit	*Chazara prieuri*
Moroccan Grayling	*Pseudochazara atlantis*
Great Sooty Satyr	*Satyrusferula atlanteus*
Giant Grayling	*Berbena abdelkader abdelkader*
False Grayling	*Arethusana arethusa dentata*

	English name	Scientific name
	Meadow Brown	*Maniola jurtina hispulla*
	Moroccan Meadow Brown	*Hyponephele maroccana maroccana*
	Moroccan Meadow Brown	*Hyponephele maroccana nivellei*
	Oriental Meadow Brown	*Hyponephele lupina mauritanica*
	Gatekeeper	*Pyronia tithonus*
	Southern Gatekeeper	*Pyronia cecilia*
	Spanish Gatekeeper	*Pyronia bathseba bathseba*
	Small Heath	*Coenonympha pamphilus pamphilus*
	Dusky Heath	*Coenonympha dorus fettigii*
	Vaucher's Heath	*Coenonympha vaucheri*
	Moroccan Pearly Heath	*Coenonympha arcanioides*
	Speckled Wood	*Pararge aegeria aegeria*
	Wall Brown	*Lasiommata megera megera*
	Large Wall Brown	*Lasiommata maera meadewaldoi*
	Plain Tiger	*Danaus chrysippus*
	Large Grizzled Skipper	*Pyrgus alveus numidus*
	Oberthur's Grizzled Skipper	*Pyrgus armoricanus maroccanus*
	Rosy Grizzled Skipper	*Pyrgus onopordi*
	Red Underwing Skipper	*Spialia sertorius ali*
	Aden Skipper	*Spialia doris*
	Sage Skipper	*Syrichtus proto*
	Barbary Skipper	*Syrichtus mohammed*
	Mallow Skipper	*Carcharodus alceae*
	Marbled Skipper	*Carcharodus lavatherae*
	Southern Marbled Skipper	*Carcharodus boeticus stauderi*
	Lulworth Skipper	*Thymelicus acteon oranus*
	Moroccan Small Skipper	*Thymelicus hamza*
	Essex Skipper	*Thymelicus lineola semicolon*
	Small Skipper	*Thymelicus flavus*
	Siver-spotted Skipper	*Hesperia comma benuncas*
	Mediterranean Skipper	*Gegenes nostrodamus*
	Pigmy skipper	*Gegenes pumilio*
	Zeller's Skipper	*Borbo borbonica*

NOTES

NOTES

NOTES

NOTES

LONDON CAMERA EXCHANGE
WINCHESTER

Established specialists for over 50 years in optical products.
Our commitment to our customers is to offer:

THE BEST ADVICE, THE BIGGEST CHOICE and THE LOWEST PRICES

Phone us last and see how we score against the rest !!

TELESCOPES   NIGHTSIGHTS

BINOCULARS   MONOCULARS   CAMERAS

CAMCORDERS   DIGITAL CAMERAS

ADVANCED PHOTO SYSTEM

COMPETITIVELY PRICED PROCESSING

15 THE SQUARE, WINCHESTER. SO23 9ES.

MAIL ORDER HOTLINE
01962 866203

FAX 01962 840978